Launch an ICO

Successful Initial Coin Offering
& Token Crowdsale: The
Complete Guide to Prepare
your Startup for Launching
Successful Initial Coin Offering,
raising Venture &
Cryptocurrency Capital

VINCENT HALE

ISBN-13: 978-1-9802-1872-2

DEDICATION

This book is dedicated to the Venture Investment Industry, which after the appearance of ICO & Crowdinvesting will never be the same

CONTENTS

ACKNOWLEDGMENTS

I express my gratitude to the three great cities on the letter M, staying in which I could find the courage to create this manual. Thanks Montreal, Minsk and Moscow

THE BASICS OF INITIAL COIN OFFERING (ICO)

Introduction to the ICO

Initial Coin Offering (ICO) is a new model for attracting investments into promising start-up projects by issuing digital tokens, distributing them among investors and then placing them on a crypto exchange.

ICO fundamentally changes the financing mechanisms by offering a quick model for raising capital.

Let's have a look at some statistics. By January 2018 there are about 370 active ICOs in the world. $ 3.1 billion dollars have been attracted with the help of ICO start-ups during 10 months this year. The 100 largest in terms of attracted funds ICOs raised $ 2.7 billion dollars with almost half of the them in the top ten rating. The fastest ICO raised $ 35 million in 24 seconds, and the largest raised more than $ 257 million over a month of activity. The most successful ICOs in terms of fundraising are Tezos which raised $ 232 million, EOS - with $ 185 million, and Bancor which raised $ 153 million in three hours.

The figures show us that the ICO is creating a new

class of securities which earlier, because of technology development simply could not exist.

Due to ICO, the company not only receives financial resources but also gains recognition in the circles of its target audience. This is because before the product enters the market, the world's leading publications will write about the company and its technologies. So, future consumers will learn about the appearance of new products.

The success of the ICO depends on the viability of the idea, the degree of the project development and the quality of marketing.

There are six stages which The ICO product goes through:

1.The development of the idea and its economic model
2.Legal detailing of the project
3.Marketing campaign
4.Technical development
5.Distribution of tokens
6.Output of tokens to the exchange

The budget for entering the ICO is 60% marketing. The main costs go to the formation of the community, working with the media and buying traffic.

ICO can be carried out independently or by passing all the processes to consulting companies. Most often, consultants are paid from Success Fee which is 10% of the collected funds plus 10% of the project's tokens.

The negative side of the transfer of ICOs to consultants is the increase of the cost of the campaign, as well as reduction of its quality. Despite the guaranteed receipt of a share from a successful ICO, the consultant is not as motivated as an entrepreneur, hence the risk to raise fewer funds, an investor is much more willing to give money to the founder of ICO rather than an intermediary.

The ideal ICO model will develop when you begin to

control training process, and consultants will be involved only for assistance in certain areas.

What will you learn from this book?

For the past 7 years we have been launching our own start-ups, developing external projects and attracting investors.

Out of the 35 ICO projects that we've considered as investors, only two showed real results.

As we attract investment, we always evaluate technology and innovation, the availability of a calculated financial and business model, traction of the team and product. Most entrepreneurs who launch ICO don't even think about these.

From this book you will learn all aspects of preparing the ICO campaign, we will start with packing ideas, team building, technical audit, building financial models, and then move on to the legal side, registering ICO and opening a bank account. After, we will consider the development of smart contracts and tokens, we will talk in detail about the promotion of the company and, in conclusion, consider the withdrawal of collected funds into your bank account.

Make your ICO successful.

ICO Dictionary. 57 important Terms

Startup is a young company that is just beginning to develop. A scalable startup has the intent to become a large company. The Intent of the startup founder is to disrupt the market with the scalable and impactful business model.

An Investor is any person who invests capital with the

expectation of financial returns.

Strategic Investor is an investor interested in acquiring a large block of shares in order to participate in the management of the company or get full control over it.

IPO is an initial public offering. it is the first time that the stock of a private company is offered to the public.

Roadshow is a series of visiting meetings of the company's management, which is going to conduct an IPO with existing and potential investors.

A security is a tradable financial asset. Securities are investments that can be traded on a secondary market.

Roadmap is a detailed plan to guide progress towards a goal.

Timeline is time schedule of the team's work on the project.

Milestones (Highlights) - a control point in project management, a significant key moment.

Venture Capital - the capital of investors, intended for financing new or growing start-ups associated with a high degree of risk.

ROI - the rate of return on investment. As a percentage shows the profitability or unprofitability of the investment of funds.

Crowdfunding is collective funding by the people who voluntarily combine their money or other resources together to support the projects of other people or organizations.

Crowdinvesting is is equity-based crowdfunding.

Blockchain - built according to certain rules, a chain of generated transaction blocks with an internal motivator for the operation of nodes.

KYC - know your customer. The term of banking and exchange regulation for financial institutions.

Fiat Money - any money declared by a government to be legal tender.

Cryptocurrency is a digital or virtual currency that uses cryptography & blockchain for security.

Token is a digital coupon that can be a substitute for money, used as a digital asset or turned on a market or a crypto exchange.

Smart-Contract is a protocol that describes a set of conditions that, on the basis of mathematical algorithms, independently conducts transactions and monitors their implementation.

Geth is the the command line interface for running a full Ethereum node.

Mist is the official Ethereum wallet which is being developed under the auspices of the Ethereum Foundation.

Token ticker is a symbol of your token, for instance BTC is the ticker for Bitcoin.

Discount - the difference between the current rate of the token and its price on the maturity date.

CAT (Custom Application Token) - an internal digital currency on the blockchain to pay for goods and services within a specific project.

Equity Token is stock token. Such tokens can be tied to the company's shares.

Token Trading Platrotms is a Digital Asset Exchange or Cryptocurrency Stock Exchange.

PreSale or also known as Pre-ICO is the token sale event that Blockchain enterprises run before the official crowdsale or ICO campaign. The fundraising targets for Pre-ICOs are often lower as compared to that of the main ICO and tokens are usually sold cheaper.

Pre-ICO is the same as PreSale.

ICO (Initial Coin Offerings) is a mechanism for attracting financing by selling future crypto currency or tokens for current, liquid crypto-currencies such as Bitcoin, Ethereum, etc. Other name is ITO / Blockchain Crowdfunding / Blockchain Crowdinvesting / CrowdSale / Token Sale.

Crowdsale - a stage of mass sale of tokens.

ITO (Initial Coin Offerings) is the same as ICO. Coins are the first generation of crypto-currency assets. The next generation of digital assets is the tokens, which covers a broader purpose of use.

Post-ICO - some activities organised after the main ICO. This can be an additional sale of tokens, or the fulfilment of commitments.

CAP - the target amount of fees for the ICO.

Soft Cap is the minimum amount required by your project on crowdsale. A synonym is Minimal Goal.

Hard Cap - is the maximum amount a crowdsale will receive.

TGE (or Token Generation Event) is an event whereby tokens are distributed to the first owners.

White Paper is a complex document that helps a potential investor to make a measured decision in favour of your company or its specific product.

Yellow Paper is a technical document describing the specific areas of your technology for evaluating the project by auditors and technology experts.

Bounty-campaign is an attraction of external outsourcing experts to ICO, carrying out a wide spectrum of work and receiving compensation for the rendered services and executed works in your tokens.

SPV (Special Purpose Vehicle) is a temporary "project company" or a special purpose company created to implement a specific project or for a specific purpose, for example, to raise funds during an ICO.

Holding is a system of commercial companies which includes «a management company» that owns controlling stakes in shares and / or shares of subsidiaries, and subsidiaries.

Ethereum is a platform for creating decentralised online services based on Blockchain.

ERC20 is the standard of interchangeable digital tokens released on Blockchain Ethereum.

HYIP (High Yield Investment Program) is a fraudulent project similar to an investment fund with high yield, a variation of the Ponzi scheme.

Scam is an attempt to defraud a person or group by gaining their confidence.

Due Diligence is a procedure for an objective independent evaluation of an investment object, including an assessment of investment risks, a comprehensive study of the company's activities, a comprehensive review of its financial condition and position on the market.

Compliance is a system of control in an organization related to compliance with legislative requirements, regulatory documents, rules and standards of supervisory bodies.

By Back is a promissory note.

Escrow is a model of account management with the involvement of a third independent party with a high reputation in the market.

MultiSig-wallet is used for Escrow. This is a wallet managed by several people at once and sending money from it is possible only with the simultaneous consent of all parties and the availability of all signatures.

MVP (Minimum Viable Product) is a product that has minimal but sufficient functions to satisfy the first users to obtain feedback from the first users and to estimate the potential of demand.

Business Plan is a statement of business goals, reasons they are attainable and plans for reaching them.

Business Model is a company's plan for generating revenues and profits. It includes the components and functions of the business including expenses.

Financial Modelling is the process of constructing an abstract representation of a real or perceived financial situation of a particular company.

Media Plan is a detailed document that determines the timing of the advertising campaign, the channels used, the basic settings and formats for advertising.

Content Marketing is a set of marketing techniques based on the creation and distribution of useful information for the consumer with the purpose of engaging and gaining trust.

Metrics are the quantifiable measures that are used to track and assess the status of a specific business process.

What is ICO (ITO), Venture Capital, Crowdinvesting & IPO?

The first ICO was held by Mastercoin in June 2013. After the Bitcointalk forum announced the launch of the project's crowdfunding. As a result, ICO Mastercoin collected more than 5 thousand bitcoins.

However, the real revolution was made by Vitalik Buterin, a Canadian of Russian origin, who needed millions of dollars to work on the Ethereum project and to collect them he decided to pre-sell the Ethereum tokens.

Preparing for ICO Ethereum, Vitalik wrote a white paper which is a document that tells potential investors about the architecture of the project, the market and the risks. A little later, crowdfunding was called ICO or crowd sale, and white paper became the standard in the industry of new crypto currency. As a result of the ICO, the Ethereum team attracted more than 31,000 bitcoins or $ 18 million at the exchange rate at the time of ICO's completion, and users purchased 60,000 project tokens-ether. Over time, the "ether" became the second in terms of the total market capitalisation of the world's crypto currency.

ICO is a mechanism for raising funds under the terms of which tokens of the future project are being sold for current liquid cryptocurrencies.

ICO is a kind of crowd-investing , therefore, investors are invited to purchase tokens or coins, which circulate within the business model of the project and are expected to grow in value while developing and scaling the project.

The goal of the ICO is to create the final product where the funds raised are invested in the development, team pay, testing, and marketing. In addition to development funds, the ICO startup also receives a community of loyal users who are able to test the products or services provided, as well as to support the project in the market.

The idea is that tokens will go up as the technology of the startup develops and within time they can be sold more expensive.

One of the conditions for launching an ICO is the startup's obligation to investors, such as:

- Redemption of a portion of the tokens sold to investors at a fixed, certainly higher price than it was on the day of the ICO;
- Sale of its services for tokens at a more favorable price;
- Payment of dividends for each token, or any other kind of bonuses that may be profitable for investors.

The distribution of tokens between the team and investors occurs after the completion of the ICO, for which a special smart-contract is created.

Initial Token Offering is more correctly called ITO, however, the term ICO is more commonly used in the market.

After the completion of the ICO, tokens begin to trade on the crypto-exchange markets and their value is formed due to supply and demand. If the project succeeds, the tokens will grow in price, sometimes quite significantly, for example, Ether, the cost of which has grown more than 300 times.

Some projects also pay a part of their profits (dividends) to the owners of the tokens on the results of their activities. This is also done using smart-contracts proportionally to the number of tokens that investors have.

Compared to the process of attracting venture capital, attracting crowd investing through ICO can be organized easier and faster. Therefore, the ICO method is quite popular today and in the future it can have an impact on the venture market as a whole.

There are indeed some parallels between the concepts of IPO and ICO. Both options for attracting investments are the sale of a part of the business to investors who see the prospect in this project and are willing to risk their money.

But ICO is not an IPO crypto option. The fundamental difference between the ICO and the traditional IPO is that IPOs are already being conducted by successful and large-scale companies, and the ICO start-up may be on the level of ideas and not even engage in any business, but the scale of its idea should turn around the situation in the world. Projects of such scale are called disruptive. Also, during the launch of ICO, digital tokens are issued instead of shares. Tokens are issued by adding transactions to the

Blockchain with their descriptions, number and unique ID.

Philosophy of investment in a Decentralized Economy

Blockchain is the main driver of decentralisation in the world. ICO is the driver of investment decentralisation, as well.

Within the ICO, companies attract investment for the implementation of projects and many investors receive cryptocurrencies or tokens, which will later be traded on exchanges and are expected to be higher than during the ICO.

Any investor wants to benefit from their investments. ICO provides an opportunity for non-professionals and small investors to receive income from early investments.

There are two types of investors, who invest into ICO:
- Investors with speculative or material motivation;
- Investors with ideological motivation.

Buying tokens released by the project after the ICO, investors expect not only to support an interesting project for themselves, but also:

- Get the benefit from reselling the tokens at a higher price in the future (assuming they will be in high demand). If the company does well, early investors can earn from x3 times to thousands of percent;
- To receive dividends from the profit of the project, a scheme for issuing dividends based on smart contracts.

Subsequently, these units can be sold on special exchanges and thus receive a return of their funds (this is the essence of the procedure of initial coin offering, or

ICO).

The price of the main tokens is tracked on exchanges on which the project has withdrawn its tokens either on the CoinMarketCap website (https://coinmarketcap.com/tokens/).

While ICO startups are still young and only a few projects have shown results, there is no need to discuss dividends yet, and today the easiest way to earn money on ICO is speculation.

Speculators buy a token cheaper, then get the profit on the growth of the token. The token is purchased at the earliest stage of PreICO when tokens are sold at a discount of 10 to 50% and then wait for the token to be released to the stock exchanges and sell when the necessary growth is achieved.

The positive side of the speculation is that at the first stage the influx of speculators attracts new investors to the project and a project has a greater chance of collecting the amount claimed.

The negative side of this model is the collapse of the price of the token which happens almost immediately after the withdrawal to the exchange since speculators start to actively get rid of tokens, and since the price of a token is formed on the basis of demand and supply, it usually falls. Together with the price of the token, the total capitalization of the startup falls, and at this point, the remaining holders of the token begin to get rid of it.

Unlike the venture market, where the investor is waiting for a financial return on investment, ICO investors do not always pursue a purely speculative goal, and sometimes finance the development of a new company in order to get something from it in the future, or invest in an idea that seems to be practically applicable and useful time-wise. Thus, investors with intangible motivation expect to take part in changing the world and use their tokens in the future, having received the services of a new project at a lower price.

So, the intangible motivation of investors is an important element in the conduct of the ICO.

Risks for investors. Models of Investment Hygiene

Why can the ICO market be dangerous for investors and how to protect yourself from uncompetitive or unfair projects?

ICO are tokens. Tokens are a promise of something in the future. Sometimes the future is defined (month, year, some event), sometimes it is not, but in any case, there are the important point for understanding:

1. Investors may lose all their invested funds (the project will be unsuccessful, it will be SCAM, there will be unforeseen circumstances with the organisers or other unforeseen circumstances will occur, such as new legislation or a new wave of economic crisis).

2. Investors may lose all their invested funds and reputation if they advise any unreliable ICO to their relatives, colleagues or friends.

3. Investors may not receive growth of assets because the management of a start-up is not able to grow from the idea of a disruptive product or service.

So, of the top five ICOs by amount of raised funds, three have gone down significantly since the offerings. EOS, which raised $ 185 million, is down 45 percent. Bancor, which collected $ 153 million, is down 47 percent, and Kin with about $ 100 million raised, is down 27 percent.

In order to reduce risks, the investor is recommended:

• Collect as much information as possible about a

startup;

- Evaluate the project and decide whether to enter ICO or not, and if so, what the budget is going to be, comparing risks and prospects;
- Accumulate key events related to the project throughout the ICO and until the very moment of entering the market;
- Decide on the strategy: exit the project or be in the project shares.

If you are an unprofessional investor, remember a number of rules of investment hygiene:

1. Invest only free funds. If you have saved money for vacation that is going to happen in two-month time, it's better not to invest. Nobody can give you a guarantee that you can return your money back.

2. Invest as much as you are ready to lose and this loss will not give you any emotional discomfort.

3. Do not invest the borrowed money since the risk of losing it is very high.

4. Distribute investments in different proportions between several ICOs.

5. Invest only in projects the economy and market of which you are aware of. If you do not understand, before investing money, research the market: what kind of companies work in it now, who generates the main profit, at what extent these companies are vulnerable.

6. Track the traction of the project team. What are the founders and advisors famous for? What positive business experience do they have?

7. Choose projects that can provide investment profit in the medium and long term, find out if they provide any bonuses, discounts, special conditions and meet your needs.

8. Determine your income - how much you want to

earn on this investment.

9. Surely, as simple as this - buy at the time of the fall and sell at the time of growth. By no means the other way around. Wait for the necessary price increase and sell half of the purchased tokens.

10. Control your excitement to invest additional funds during the boom in the price of the token.

With such approach, it's impossible to make millions. But remember the crises of 2007-2009, 1929-1939 and dozens of others. They made happy several, and miserable - millions.

The basics of Crowdsale Business Model

Now that you have a general idea of what ICO is, we'll talk about the main points of the ICO campaign model.

The most important thing in ICO is a new idea about the future breakthrough product. The idea should be economically sound, scalable and it must have a promising and growing market.

To pack ideas, the team works through an economic model and develops "rules of the game" for investors, determining how the token is used in the system, what services can be purchased for this token, and why the demand for these services will grow in the future. In other words, why an investor should be interested to invest into this project.

The essence of ICO is the release of tokens for a future project with a target to sell them to investors.

At the end of the investment period, the ICO organizer distributes the tokens proportionally among investors. In most cases, such tokens can be used in the project itself or be a source of profit from the share of capital. Sometimes tokens can act as real shares.

It is assumed that the received by the investors tokens

can be resold at a higher price on exchanges or receive dividends on them. A lot of organizers of ICO suggest that Token Sale is the last stage of the ICO. That's why we see so many non-viable ICO projects.

The ICO model will be able to develop steadily if the team launches a successful profitable project with the money it gets from the ICO. Part of the profit will be directed to the redemption of its token with a view to its repayment. In this case, the system will be returnable - entrepreneurs will receive an investment tool and investors will get return on investment. For example, you can decree the redemption of 30% of tokens 18 months after the completion of the ICO, and on a monthly basis allocate 10% of the profit for the redemption of the remaining tokens.

Normally, the exchange value of tokens depends on the success of the project, although directly the token rate is NOT tied to the company's value and depends on supply and demand. But if a startup earns and grows its capitalization, investors get a meaningful profit, and if they do not, the ICO members do not receive anything other than non-convertible electronic coins.

FOUNDAMENTALS & ECONOMIC OF THE ICO

Tokens and Digital Assets

A token in a Blockchain is a crypto currency which is the equivalent of a unit of a financial instrument that is represented on a crypto exchange. During the ICO tokens are sold to investors in exchange for other crypto-currencies or fiat money.

Tokens are a new class of digital assets that can denote debt obligations, ownership rights, shares, bonds, movie tickets, the domestic currency of different systems and even live geese!

Tokens can be programmed to be anything:

- Digital coupon;
- Option;
- Means of payment;
- Access (for example, beta access to an online game) ;
- Internal or universal unit of account (crypto-dollars and crypto-gold on different exchanges) ;

- Service;
- Bonus;
- Discount, etc.

At the same time, several types of tokens can be used in one project, for example:

- Internal technical token, which has no name, and is used only for transactions in the block chain system;
- The share for which the dividends are paid from the operation of the system;
- Internal currency for settlements within the system.
- Motivational tokens for participants;
- A separate currency that can be exchanged on external exchanges.

Among the most common types of tokens are the following:

- Equity tokens which represent the company's shares.
- Utility tokens. They reflect some value within the business model of the online platform (reputation, scores for certain actions, game currency) ;
- Asset-backed tokens. These are digital obligations for real goods or services (kilograms of corn, an hour of the designer's work, etc.);
- Appcoins or In-Platform ones;
- Debt tokens (they are also called credit tokens) ;
- Mix-models and others.

Each token can perform one or more functions:

- The Share in a particular start-up.
- It can be used as an Accounting tool (number of API calls, upload volume on torrents).

- Digital Assets which is digital ownership of land or potatoes in a warehouse.
- A method of rewarding the miners, as in Bitcoin.
- A way to prevent attacks.
- The currency which is the means of payment between the participants.
- Fee for using the system.

At the moment, there are no established standards for the functioning of the token in a particular project, so it is indicated in each offer individually. Also, the offer specifies the type of the token and describes all the rights that this token possesses.

The main parameters of the token that you need to consider are:

- Asset Title - the name of your token;
- Description - Short description or tagline (about 100 characters);
- Symbol - Token / coin ticker (BTC, for example);
- Platform - Ethereum, Waves, NEM etc. or your own;
- Price of one Token;
- CAP - is equal to the received amount in USD.

There are 3 basic types of tokens:

- Tokens-shares;
- Credit tokens;
- Appcoins.

Tokens-shares are used to finance development and build a network. They are not needed to access the company's services. In fact, they can be considered as crypto-shares of the company.

In exchange for investment, holders of stock tokens receive dividends in the form of interest on income or part of commissions for transactions in the network.

In many cases, stock tokens are shares in organisations such as DAO. In these structures, the program code releases tokens, collects money from the sale of tokens, and makes contracts with development companies.

In addition to receiving the reward, holders of DAO tokens also vote on investment proposals of companies. The number of votes is proportional to the package of stock tokens.

Credit tokens can be considered as short-term loans to the network in exchange for interest income from the loan amount. One of the first networks using credit tokens became the Steemit network. After the completion of the ICO, the project implementation phase follows.

Appcoins is a digital currency that gives access to the services that a distributed network provides. An analogue of an app coin is a token for visiting an attraction.

You can earn tokens by creating values in the corresponding network. In networks of Bitcoin, Ethereum you can be engaged in mining and in the network such as Steemit tokens can be earned as a result of mining as well as publishing content that is in demand. Since tokens are written in the Blockchain, they can be freely bought and sold for any crypto currency or for fiat money.

Primary cost of one Token, Internal Value & Number of Tokens Issued for ICO

The Internal Value of the Token is determined based on the specifics of the project being launched and its technology. For example, at the stage of launching an ICO, one token can be equal to one dollar of debt, one stock of the company, one kilogram of cucumbers, or 10 shares of the company, the right to vote anywhere, or anything really.

How much should one token cost? You can only guess how much one token will actually cost since the final cost will depend on the amount of fees at the end of the ICO.

The real value of the token will be determined by the market when it is put on the stock exchange. You can determine how much presumably one token is during the ICO before entering the exchange.

How to do it?

Imagine that you have already launched the ICO and have already collected funds for 3 days and have now collected Ether & Bitcoin for a total of $2.5 million in a fiat-equivalent.

Let's suppose you issue 100 million tokens, 85 million of which will be distributed among investors and the rest are reserved for the development of the project.

In total, by the third day of ICO we calculate the cost of one token as follows: $85000000/2500000 = 34$ for 1 dollar.

Then, divide the total number of tokens sold into the collected amount and get the number of tokens, equal to the value of one dollar $(1/34 = 0.0294117647)$.

After, divide one dollar into the resulting number and get the cost of one token, which is a little less than three cents.

However, the price of a token will gradually increase because during the ICO more and more investments will be attracted, which means that the number of tokens that investors receive will be adjusted accordingly.

How many tokens to release? For the convenience of calculations during the ICO, you need to release millions of tokens. Since millions of dollars are collected on the ICO and each token has a high growth potential, it is necessary that the total amount be multi-million. For example, Bitcoin is also the token. Now in the world there are 16.7 million bitcoins, and there will be about 21 million of them in total.

You can take an equal amount for the count, for example 30, 70 or 100 millions of tokens. It is important to understand that the issue of each token has its own cost, therefore, it makes sense to emit too large multibillion volumes of tokens only when it is caused by organizational necessity. In case you do not know where you can use a Blockchain or a token, then pass the development of the concept of the token and the inclusion of the block to external consultants.

Pre-Sale of Crypto Tokens

The mechanism for pre-selling tokens directly depends on the type of tokens. The sequence of actions in the preliminary sale of stock tokens:

1. The Publication of the network description and plans for further development (White paper).
2. The creation of a smart contract with a number of token-shares reserved for the founders of the network.
3. The creation of a provider company that will develop the network for a fee.
4. Advertising and promotion of the forthcoming ICO and the sale of token shares to all comers. From the money received you should make a payment to the provider company.
5. Work on the expansion of the network, collection and distribution of reward for the use of the network.

Crowdsale. Appcoins Sale

The sequence of actions in pre-selling tokens is the following:

1. Publication of the network description and plans for further development (White paper).

2. Announcement of the forthcoming ICO and publication of the source code before the generation of the first token.

3. Deploying the network and generating tokens with the help of mining. It is possible to reserve part of the tokens for the founders, as a reward for the idea and development of the network.

4. ICO advertising and the sale of tokens to all comers.

5. Work to create a network effect, creation of applications and support of the network. As the network grows, the demand for tokens increases, which leads to an increase in the cost of user tokens.

Models of Smart Contracts

Blockchain also allows you to systematize the legal procedure and transfer its execution to algorithms which are called Smart Contracts.

Smart Contract is a software algorithm that describes a set of conditions, the performance of which automatically occurs in the real world or digital systems.

At the heart of a smart-contract is a class condition: IF - ELSE. Based on this, you can program a smart-contract for anything. For example, if the temperature outside falls below 10 degrees Celsius, then 100 euros is automatically transferred from your account to support an animal shelter or to form a smart-contract of the Fund, in which the percent of the profit of the project is automatically sent for further purchase of Tokens.

Any condition can be laid into a smart contract and it will be executed.

The classic ICO smart contract looks like this: investors automatically receive tokens to their wallets, depending on the volume of the invested funds.

Smart contracts are capable of:

- Functioning as accounts with a «multi-signature», so that the funds will be withdrawn only if the transaction is confirmed by a certain percentage of people who have access to account management;
- Monitoring the implementation of agreements concluded between users, for example, an insurance contract, and providing conditions for the performance of other contracts (similar to how libraries of program modules work);
- Storing information about the application. For instance, domain registration information or a database of registered users.

The smart-contracts models can be categorized as follows:

- Joint smart-contract which manage shares and stakes held by shareholders;
- Credit agreements;
- Corporate smart-contracts where the participants agree on specific actions to implement the rights of the corporation;
- Labor and salary smart-contracts;
- Agreements of a civil-law nature (aimed at the emergence, modification or termination of mutual rights and obligations) ;
- Property (purchase, sale, lease, transfer into partial ownership) ;
- Insurance (insurance of crypto-currency accounts, transactions, hedging of risks) ;

- Agency agreements;
- Smart contracts of commercial concession (franchise or royalty);
- Trust Management Contracts;
- Banking tools (derivatives, escrow, collection, letter of credit).

One of the most common of mentioned above is a Profit sharing contract. That is an agreement on the sharing of profits between the owner of assets and a person actually managing these assets, which determines the order in which the profit from the use of these assets will be divided between the parties.

BEFORE THE ICO

Ideal ICO

In order to successfully conduct the ICO, at least two months of preparation is required, but 5 is even better. It is advisable not to hurry because reducing the deadlines reduces the quality of training, which can certainly affect the results of fees.

In order to conduct an "ideal" ICO, you should have the following:

1. Confirmed viability of a business idea.
2. Protection of investors from fraud.
3. Tested technology.
4. Rational use of financing for minimum and maximum indicators of collected funds.
5. The established regulatory framework.
6. Transparency of ICO.
7. Managed expenditure of financing.
8. Deferred liquidity for the project creators.

9. The presence of experienced members in the team that have already brought projects into the global market.

Before you start to conduct an ICO, you first need to study the market so that you, as founders, personally see the level of quality that you need to maintain. In order to do it you should:

1. Learn which projects have recently effectively conducted ICO. Of the latest successful ICOs, I recommend looking at Civic, EOS, Polybius. Study their websites, the branches on the BitcoinTalk forum, what media they were discussed in, the content and quality of the articles, study their activity and audience response in social networks, download Whitepaper from the sites of these projects, read the FAQ, join their public chat rooms. You need to immerse yourself in this environment, start thinking in cryptology.

2. Examine the competitors. Projects compete for the money of investors, therefore, your competitors are not only potential thematic competitors in your niche, but also other ICOs that will go in parallel with your ICO. They are all different, many have much to learn from.

With an ideal ICO model, a clean project should take care of the following:

- You should prove to potential investors the validity of the ICO and the soundness of issuing your own crypto currency.
- Disclose plans for the development of the project and conduct an open dialogue with potential investors.
- Implement a test version of your own protocol before

ICO.

- Provide the possibility of direct "miming" currencies to involve new users and provide the network with the necessary resources to process transactions.
- Enter ICO with a clear understanding of how much investment you need to attract.
- Have an agreement with a specific exchange to issue tokens.
- The founding team should own between 10% and 50% of all tokens and should not exchange them during the first three years of operation.

Analysis of failed ICOs. Possible Mistakes in preparation for the ICO

The huge success of individual ICOs has strengthened others in the view that it is easy to raise funds through the ICO. It's a delusion. ICO is not a way to earn easy money. Attracting funding from strangers is difficult and it should be so.

For several months, we have witnessed the creation and launch of many ICO projects. Some of them ended successfully, collecting the necessary amount. Others have experienced some difficulties in attracting capital.

When conducting an ICO, it is difficult to avoid mistakes, so I'll focus your attention on the main points faced by projects that were in my orbit.

The main criteria are reduced to the evaluation of the success of the four main

elements:

- Viability of a business idea and the potential market
- Team
- Technology
- The mechanism of crowdfunding.

The rest is reliability, security and reputation. It will be an additional guarantee for investors, but only if you are all right with the basic characteristics.

So, what factors distinguish successful ICOs from unsuccessful ones?

- Unworked legal model, especially with regard to company registration, the withdrawal of tokens into Fiat money. Be sure to consult a lawyer in this case!
- In addition to legal and tax consequences, the worst thing that can happen with your ICO is accusations in the scam (scam - slang means any negative phenomenon). Reputation is very important. Constantly ask yourself the question: can anything I write or make cause charges in the scam.
- Unprocessed or unviable idea.
- Unprocessed technical part in the field of cybersecurity, as a result of which tokens and raised funds become vulnerable to hackers. Get experts on cybersecurity.
- It is difficult for a small team to do all the work. You draw money from investors for a future product, so involve the team for future incomes. Be sure to delegate tasks to reliable performers, do not try to grasp the immensity. It is important not to stretch the training process in time and not to lose sight of important points.
- Technical implementation must be thought over from and to. A considerable part of investors will want to take part in your project, having only fiat money in their hands. It means, to get a wallet and to acquire a crypto currency for some is a difficult task. So, it is important to take this into account and think over every detail: write down all the instructions and

prepare big investors for pre-ICO in advance.

- Correct definition of terms is also important. This characteristic is difficult to calculate, but it depends on the timing of whether the ICO will reach the ceiling or barely get to the bottom.
- Be prepared for complex questions about your project. In the crypto community there are advanced people and if they consider you incompetent, you will not be able to earn their trust.
- Users can be different: scammers can come and start publishing fishing links. Moderate all channels, preferably around the clock. During the ICO, this is especially recommended: a link from a user with a nickname like MainModerator, which will hang overnight in your channels, can significantly impair your reputation.

What Problems can arise with the Business Idea:

- The lack of a clear market and clear business orientations;
- A limited or unknown market and an undefined business plan.

The Key problems with the team can be:

- Unconfirmed and not showing its ability to implement projects;
- Uncertain team composition and management structure;
- Evidence that the developers were involved in fraudulent activities in the past.

Tested technology:

- A lack of confirmation of the working capacity of the concept and other technical inspections;
- Incomplete technology and lack of confirmation of the concept;

- Interruptions in the technical work of the main ICO platform.

The mechanism of crowdfunding:
- Poorly planned ICO in terms of investor protection.
- Large-scale bonus program for the first participants.
- A bonus program, according to which from the first day until the goal was reached, 50% of the investment was returned, along with a declining exchange rate.

The above projects are just a few examples, which we hope, quite clearly illustrate the main causes of the problems that ICO faces.

Does your company need ICO?

The excitement of ICO is so high that in a matter of minutes the campaigns are over, collecting millions, tens or hundreds of millions of dollars. Such success doesn't leave people indifferent, which leads to the desire to hold their own ICO.

Despite the hype around the ICO and the prospects of a release from the captivity of venture capital, it is worth asking yourself four questions:

1. Is it just for the sake of money that you want to hold an ICO? What other expectations do you have?
2. Do you need ICO with your own or existing crypto currency, which your project will be tied up to?
3. What are your threats with an unsuccessful ICO?
4. Does your project have sufficient countermeasures against systematic risks?

You have a chance to release your own token and hope for its viability and profitability in the long term.

Remember and consider the tips before proceeding to the action. The main aspects that you should think about before launching ICO are:

Do you have a good project? Does it really have the potential to revolutionize and change the world?

The intrinsic value of the token. Why does the project need Blockchain tokens? How to connect the Blockchain-token with the product functionally? How does the token work within the platform or technology? As the founder of Ethereum Vitalik Buterin said "If you can manage without a token, then ICO is not necessary.»

Blockchain is the basis of technology. Does your product need Blockchain? What advantages can Blockchain technology give to your product? How is Blockchain used? Previously, having your Blockchain was the main rule, now it's not necessary. Today, you can sell digital vouchers, equivalent to the cost of electricity generated by your company, for example.

Are you able to be completely open to the community and are you ready for the full transparency of your life for the next few years?

How can your token be of interest to investors? Is there a mechanism that links its value to the success of your product?

Does the profit distribution model contribute to the joint enrichment of developers and investors after the ICO? Is distribution fair?

Will it comply with your current laws? Have you received confirmation of the legality of your scheme from a lawyer? Read about Howie criteria.

Do you have the initial means to launch the ICO?

Sometimes it is better to evaluate everything properly, weigh risks and abandon the plans, rather than suffer reputational costs or get suits for violating the law.

Be very careful with ideas in which you sell a stake in

your company or make any forecasts about the profits of your investors, in some cases such projects fall under the regulation of the Securities And Exchange Commission (SEC), where the procedure is significantly more complicated in comparison with the usual ICO and more resembles an IPO.

ICO SCAM & Anti-Fraud

Only a few investors have enough knowledge and information to make conscious decisions and understand the uniqueness of the technology and its token underlying the project. Unprofessional investors blindly finance projects in anticipation of a long-term, cost-effective and freely convertible digital asset at the crypto-exchange.

It is often used by some unscrupulous ICO-creators who launch deliberately false and fraudulent projects on 100% Crowdsale. Because of the high hype of ICO, it is not known what a project really is. A huge part of the projects are just beautiful pictures and ideas, some of which are not viable and can not work in principle. They promise investors the launch of a new breakthrough project or a unique crypto currency, but after raising funds, scammers do not hold back to promises and leave with money received.

And although the majority of ICOs conducted do not have bad intentions, this situation is reflected in the entire cryptocurrency market, and the activities of scammers are forcing the community to be more cautious, and investors are becoming more cautious about the next "technological revolution».

Such a situation can lead to the catastrophe of the entire ICO market, when investors will resolutely reject new ICO-projects, backed up by really good ideas.

A brief overview of the basic tricks of ICO fraud:

- ICO project for the creation of only a digital currency, which is positioned as a universal means for international payments without indicating its specific advantages.
- Developers are throwing all their efforts to promote the project, while almost no-one talks about technical development and the code.
- The project promises huge figures on profitability or a multiple increase in the value of the token.
- It is announced about the development of platform technology, while the results of work are not shown, and the code is not laid out on GitHub.
- The project does not have an explicit model for using the token, and at the same time R&D is announced and money is needed to develop hardware technology.
- Project developers or team members are notorious in professional circles or have already been involved in dark matters.

How much does ICO cost? Planning ICO Budget

As early as the beginning of 2017, ICO did not require significant funds and startups held ICO spent about $ 10-20k on preparation. Today, the price of holding an ICO is constantly growing. This is due to the appearance of expensive intermediaries in the market, and the fact that the number of ICO projects is growing as an avalanche, however the number of investors is growing at a much slower rate. So, to attract the attention of investors with each new ICO, the costs of marketing and traffic are becoming more expensive.

The budget for the ICO is approximately 60% of the

cost of promotion. The main expenses are spent on forming a community around the project, working with the media and buying traffic.

According to the estimates of consultants, the average cost of collecting $ 1mln is $ 35-45k, but there are cases when 1mln projects spend 200k for collecting. Everything depends very much on the niche, on the experience of entrepreneurs, the scope of the project idea, the experience of consultants and good understanding of the project development strategy. Some projects manage to collect $ 400k with only $ 5k spent.

With the right strategy and proper preparation, it takes about $ 150-250k to collect $ 5-6 million. On a case-by-case basis, this figure varies, and I saw several ICOs which ultimately spent more than they collected in the end. This happens, just it is not written on news sites about these ICOs and they are not added to the portfolio of consultants.

On average, ICO with external consultants costs from $ 50 to $ 700 thousand, the figure depends on the depth of involvement of outside consultants in your project. Maybe someone takes even more expensive, but I have not met such.

Before starting an ICO, you need to know the exact amount that you need to collect to successfully implement the project. If the ICO budget is incorrectly calculated, you may face 2 problems:

1. You can underestimate the scale of the costs necessary for spending and the entire ICO process will be disrupted.
2. If you conduct a Pre-ICO for an ICO, and you overstate Pre-Sale financing, it is likely that primary investors will suspect your project in SCAM.

Therefore, it is important to understand exactly how much you need at each stage of preparation.

Pre-ICO, ICO, Post-ICO

So, knowing how much money is needed to fully conduct an ICO, the question arises within a start up: where to get $ 30, $ 50 or $ 200k to conduct an ICO?

Now, there are more and more projects that run a preliminary fund-raising (Pre-ICO) to raise money for marketing, participants' salaries and other expenses before the main ICO.

When a promising project aimed at changing the world does not have enough funds for ICO, start-ups attract primary investors to finance site development, company registration, legal fees, marketing and other expenses necessary for ICO. Pre-ICO is also called Pre-Sale. This approach is similar to how banks and financial institutions lend to companies preparing an IPO.

During the Pre-ICO, the start-up raises funds solely for the main ICO. Investors financing the project at this stage will receive a token with the maximum discount, and the startup will have the opportunity for the proper conduct of the ICO campaign and funding for the next half year of preparation. On average, the duration of the Pre-ICO is about a month, and projects at this stage collect from $ 30k to $ 200k.

Pre-ICO can be open to the entire market, or closed, when by using promotion you codes invite a limited circle of participants to become your first investors.
At this stage, the startup draws out the concept of a breakthrough idea, determines the start date of the Pre-

ICO and ICO, the amount of funding, the duration of fundraising, the number of tokens produced, determines other details and makes the announcement of the Pre-ICO.

I want to note that the Pre-ICO is a non-binding step, and it fits projects that do not have primary funding. Typically, if a company conducting an ICO has an existing business, the Pre-ICO stage is skipped and the company goes directly to the ICO.

By conducting pre-sale and pre-ICO, you can decide to release tokens only at the end of the main round of investment after the ICO.

Once you have collected funds during Pre-Sale, the project team proceeds to the ICO stage. During the ICO, the project collects funds to develop the technology of its product, to support the team, to bring this technology to the global market and all related costs. This stage is the main one in attracting funding for the entire life cycle of your project.

Then comes Post-ICO, which is the main stage of production of your product and fulfillment of obligations to investors. Sometimes at this stage it is possible to conduct additional fundraising, but in this case it should be announced once in the road map before the Pre-ICO.

Geography of ICO

When planning an ICO, you need to immediately determine the geography of attracting your investors. Local ICOs promoted only in one country rarely collect the expected funds in the right amount.

Another weighty reason why it is necessary to launch an ICO of a global scale is the global scale of technological revolutions, and the funding of world-class projects rather than regional ones by investors.

But be careful, citizens of some countries, such as citizens of Singapore, the United States and some others, can not sell tokens. You should study this question yourself at the time of preparation of your ICO.

The main language for ICO is English. It will be a good idea to make language localization in Spanish, Chinese, Russian, French, German, Japanese, Portuguese and Dutch, so you will increase organic traffic and will attract the attention of non-professional investors who do not speak English, to your ICO, and there are many such in the world, especially in the Asian region.

Life after ICO & Fulfillment of Commitments

When the organizers are super focused on the launch of the ICO, very few people think what will happen next.

Most investors buy tokens on the ICO in order to later sell them at a higher price. Few people are waiting for the achievement of milestones from "White Paper". Investors want the growth rate. At the current stage of market development, this is normal.

But despite the lack of motivation among the investors, the startup has a number of obligations at the end of the ICO.

The main problem about which almost no one thinks is: what will happen to the business at the end of the road. Logically there are 2 positive scenarios:

- The team conducts a real IPO;
- The team sells its stake to a strategic investor, usually a larger industry company.

But with 10 thousand unknown investors you can not hold an IPO. That's why it's important to determine with Know Your Customer (KYC) from the very beginning. Yes, at the preparation stage this reduces the conversion fees, most users want to speculate anonymously. But if your technology really has a huge market potential to be the next Unicorn, you must foresee this step.

The fulfillment of obligations, upon completion of the fees, the startup should:

1. Conduct an internal audit of the ICO, and reconcile the accrued tokens with the received money.
2. If the offer provided excess tokens, you need to burn all the extra tokens.
3. Accrue tokens to investors.
4. Distribute tokens for bounty-campaign.
5. Put tokens on stock exchanges.
6. Form the team, hiring the necessary for the development of technology specialists and get involved in the development.

You must remember that one of your most basic tasks is to match the terms of milestones described in the road map and White Paper. Another important task after the ICO is to keep in touch, several times a week inform the community about the news of the project and its development in all blogs.

PREPARING YOUR STARTUP FOR AN ICO

Conditions for ICO investors. 20 Tips

In order for investors to see the interest of your project, they need to develop an economic justification and rules for the game, why a token is needed in this product, what services can be purchased for this token, how the project will develop and why the demand for these services will increase. In other words, why should a rational investor should invest in this project.

It is important to define all the conditions:

1. Decide on the duration of the ICO. Do not delay the time, one month is enough. Some projects needed 15 minutes.
2. Determine the start and end date of the Pre-ICO / ICO.
3. Determine the amount of discount for the first investors. This is called a "price ladder". Early buyers of tokens receive a discount in reward for being "on board" first. Usually the Crowdsale set a bonus of 20-

41

25%.

4. Decide whether to conduct Pre-ICO.
5. What currencies are accepted by Bitcoin, Ethereum? Will you sell a token for Fiat? If so, how will it buy a token for Fiat?
6. Which platform will the tokens be issued on?
7. Pre-ICO: what will the first investors receive and on what terms? How many tokens are already released, how many are sold and how many will be released?
8. Decide on the number of released and mined tokens, is there a limit on release, how to determine the initial price of the tokens, what will happen to the unsold tokens?
9. How many of the tokens are to the team, how many to ICO, how many on bounty-activity. Is the distribution automatic, through smart contracts or manual?
10. What are the conditions of a bounty program?
11. Is there a maximum hidden cap that stops collecting funds.
12. Funds received.
13. Motivation for investing: participation in profits, sale on the exchange, participation in management? Is it a long-term investment or a short-term investment?
14. At what amount of funds is the campaign considered successful? Is there a return if the goal is not reached?
15. After the completion of the ICO: where will the collected funds go? Are there different types of development depending on the money collected?
16. With which exchanges have preliminary agreements been reached on listing the token and what are the listing terms?
17. Who are mentors, advisors, project experts?
18. Conduct audit of the source code by independent auditors, confirm the availability of source code on GitHub.
19. For citizens of the United States and other countries: are they making investments?

20. Is there an Escrow (guarantors with access to the collected funds)?

Make a page on the Guide website where you describe «How to participate in the Your Token Sale».

Milestones, Roadmap & Development Plan

The plan for the development of a new product or project is an integral part of the ICO. You can draw the key points from this plan, such as - milestones, which are the underlying part of the Roadmap project.

Roadmap is convenient for perception by potential investors, because visually comfortable infographics reflects each highlight of the development of the project.

Roadmap is done immediately for the entire project, and it includes the stages of:

- Pre-ICO;
- ICO;
- Development of Smart-Contract;
- Output of the token on the exchange;
- Development of technology;
- Creation of MVP;
- Product creation;
- Launch of the project to the market;
- Promotion;
- Achievement of KPI;
- Development Plan.

Such stages of preparation as the study of the economic model, all kinds of analysis, the construction of the financial model and other preparatory blocks in the roadmap should not be detailed, but it's better to refer them to one item "strategic planning».

The general plan for creating a new project looks roughly the following way.

1. Preparation:

- Idea and its packaging;
- Evaluation of the market (with the study of the target audience) ;
- The concept of business (which is a description of the initial hypotheses about the future business, its goals: what, why and who to create for) ;
- Team building with burning eyes and high potential;
- Set of the technical task.

2. Development:

- Creating a prototype or MVP;
- Testing;
- Alpha version;
- Closed Beta;
- Public beta.

3. Promotion:

- Launch;
- Promotion;
- Scaling, development and global expansion.

Everything that concerns the development and promotion blocks can be in your roadmap. Also, in roadmap you can specify such items as: full launch of the site, launch of the mobile application, launch the project at full power, connection with key partners, and others.

ICO Campaign Plan and Timeline

If Roadmap reflects your overall project vision, Timeline shows investors exactly when the ICO process will take place, the distribution of tokens and their subsequent withdrawal to the stock exchange. Timeline can include the Pre-ICO, ICO and Post-ICO stages (if you plan to raise funds after the completion of the ICO).

In terms of deadlines: for a successful ICO, at least two months of preparation is required, but it is advisable to allocate from 5 to 6 months. Even in this period with having the right team, the preparation will be quite dense. To prepare in 2 months you have to greatly expand the team, and practically do not sleep. Therefore, the first Timeline point should not be earlier than 2 months, for this.

You can not allocate Timeline into one category, so that investors do not confuse Roadmap and Timeline. Just add information with a vision of the development of the ICO campaign.

In the ICO Timeline, you need to specify:

- Start and end dates of Pre-ICO
- The Start date of the Crowdsale
- Dates of increase in the cost of tokens
- Date of distribution of tokens between investors

Startup Team and External Advisors

If investors like the idea and the economy of the ICO project, then the second thing they look at is the team who will implement the new project.

The investor appreciates the transparency, experience and sanity of the founders, therefore, the mandatory condition for trust is the disclosure of key project participants. The team should be ready to show their faces, publish personal data, talk about their experience, the progress of the project.

If the project exists only at the level of the idea, then it is possible to raise significant funds only under the condition of unquestionable authority of the initiators of the project. There must be an expert in the team, whose name is known either in the whole world or in the field of crypto finances.

The ICO market is now overheated, therefore it's unlikely that you will be able to collect two dozen people in one place, so you should try to work with remote employees. Use Google Drive, Trello, Slack, Google Hangouts and other tools for teamwork.

Investors evaluate:

- The professionalism of the team and the ability to implement the project;
- Openness - all team members will be closely examined;
- The background of the team and the project itself;
- Experience and history should be not only successful, but also relevant to industry applications;
- Working with the community - it's important to be transparent and always in touch.

The minimum amount of people who need to conduct an ICO is:

- The project manager. A person who looks after

everything and is responsible for ensuring that all work is done well;

- 2 community managers. Those are managers who 24/7 answer all questions in all public communication Channels;
- 1 bounty-manager who is the leader of the bounty-program, they can be combined with the community-manager;
- PR-specialist, the manager who works with the media;
- Editor. You will need a lot of texts in the blog and the media about your product and the market you want to go to, also you need to cover all the ICO news in great detail, this will require a good editor;
- SMM-specialists in context and targeting, who are buying traffic from Facebook, Google, Reddit, Youtube;
- Designer for the website and all related materials;
- Programmer of the site, programmer of smart contacts and tokens;
- A number of specialists who are involved in point tasks such as developing an ICO site, design, etc.

You must calculate the team's payment from two to six months of preparation for the ICO, and two to eight weeks of the ICO phase itself. Totally about 8 months of work.

You can use own or borrowed funds to pay team for work or the PRE ICO funds, as well.

It is possible to work on a model when you pay a small salary to each employee and provide an option with the condition of a large bonus on the basis of ICO (from three to ten salaries).

Also for the ICO, lawyers, external consultants, and interpreters are required. When you gather an excellent team, to solve technical and legal issues, I strongly recommend that you recruit specialists for consultations.

Registration of companies, taxes, withdrawal of fiat money, editing of White Paper, security of tokens, responsibility to investors - all this should be thought through by specialists to the smallest detail.

As a reward, consultants charge a commission for services as a percentage of issued tokens.

Another of the most important goals of the team's formation is to get the support of the project among famous people in the world of crypto-currencies. You should get Advisers' help with the promotion of your ICO by speaking at forums, conferences, in their blogs and elsewhere. To keep them motivated, it is recommended not to pay until the completion of ICO and keep their motivation due to more successful release of tokens.

Ideally, you need the following types of advisers:

4. 1.Blockchain adviser
3. Branch advisers
4. Marketing adviser
5. Legal adviser
6. US adviser
7. China adviser
8. Korean adviser
9. EU adviser
10. Financial adviser

Financial, Marketing and Business Plan Outline

At the heart of any business is the model of making money. In order to understand how many funds must be collected to create and develop the project, it is necessary to calculate the financial needs of the company for the coming years.

The total amount of such needs will express the

minimum amount of ICO Crowdsale - Soft Cap. Financial needs of the company are calculated in the financial plan or financial model of the project.

In theory any money can be "raised" during the ICO. But for the start of a serious technological project, an amount that is more than $ 3 million dollars is rarely required. In addition, the collected amounts should always be justified.

The financial model is a business X-ray, it shows the financial framework of your project. The financial model is a reflection of the business model. The model consists of a system of interrelated indicators of all components of the business, expressed in quantitative units of measure (money, interest, people, things, days, months).

For most ICO startups, it is sufficient to model the operating activities and cash flow. But if the technology development takes more than 12 months, calculate the full version of the financial model, which will take into account all aspects of the future business.

To build a financial model, you need to take into account:
- Economic environment (inflation, taxes)
- R&D and Sales;
- The number of employees and their salaries;
- Current costs (including material, production, administrative, commercial, cost, advance payments and accounts payable);
- Working capital, current assets and liabilities;
- Sources of financing (investment loans, loans).

As a result of the interaction of all these indicators, you have a general picture of the business, which sometimes shows that the analysed company can become financially insolvent in the next 18 months.

If you have never developed financial models, review a separate course on financial modeling, then develop a draft of the financial model yourself, and then involve the expert in the financial modeling for finalizing.

Things to consider while doing it:
- In the financial model, you should consider the development of exactly the technology which functions are announced to your ICO investors;
- Do not forget to take into account the costs of Ethereum Gaz;
- Do think about the high expenditure of ICO costs - so that it does not happen that 1/3 of the product development money is spent on marketing the ICO campaign;
- Put costs on the Bounty Campaign;
- Remember about the possible reverse buy-out of the token from investors;
- Analyze the cost of Blockchain & IT specialists for R&D.

In addition, determine the minimum amount to start the project - Soft Cap, and the maximum amount - Hard Cap. Show investors what costs you will cover when you collect more of the claimed Soft Cap.

Attraction of Investors and Model of distribution of Tokens

As in the venture market, it is necessary to attract primary investors with large capitals to conduct an ICO.

This is one of the most important parts of the ICO,

because usually half or even most of the tokens are bought by a small number of large investors, while the other half or a smaller part is sold in retail and remains in the team.

Negotiations with large ICO investors need to start long before the ICO itself. Such negotiations somewhat resemble holding a roadshow in the organization of large companies' IPOs. During this period, a company that is going to become public travels to cities and meets with large investors to demonstrate the benefits of investing in this company's shares. It's the same in ICO: even before its launch it is necessary to begin attracting strategic investors to your ICO.

Who can this be:

- Venture funds that experiment with investments in ICO projects;
- Crypto-currency investment funds;
- Entrepreneurs who have recently organized a successful ICO.

I will reveal a little secret. In the Crowdsale market, very often the same money is used to reinvest in other ICOs. This is due to the fact that entrepreneurs collecting CAP themselves become investors for the purpose of speculation on someone else's tokens.

Prepare for negotiations with strategic investors: form an investment memorandum and a model for the distribution of tokens.

This might look like this:

- 5% of tokens remain at the board of directors
- 13% of the tokens go to the project team

- 40% to large investors
- 30% of tokens go to open market
- 2% of tokens on Bounty
- 10% of tokens remain in reserve for additional capitalization (for example).

Bounty campaign

Bounty is the reward to users for various activities: PR-promotion, activity on forums, maintenance of topics in local language versions, translation of documents into other languages, publications in social networks, blogs and so on.

For a start-up, Bounty is an opportunity to get from the specialists necessary expenses for the creation and promotion of ICO services, and at the same time save before the ICO on primary expenses.

Bounty for a specialist is an opportunity to earn tokens of a prospective project for certain advertising and information activities without having to invest their money. For each task, the bounty-specialist receives a certain reward in the form of promises for tokens. These tokens can be exchanged for other crypto-currencies after the completion of the ICO campaign.

The model is as follows: from the general list of works you select those works, to the realization of which you attract bounty specialists. Next, you select the number of tokens, send them to bounty, for instance, let's take 1 million tokens. Then you assign the cost of payment for each type of work.

Popular types of bounty tasks are:

- graphic design of logos, presentations, booklets and other information (sometimes on a competitive basis);
- translations of ICO information into other languages;
- creation of videos;
- Facebook & Twitter campaigns;
- PR campaigns;
- subscription campaigns at the BitcoinTalk Forum;
- posting information about the project in instant messengers;
- search for bugs;
- development of mobile applications, wallets or other software add-ins;
- placement in ICO sheets;
- placing information about the project on Youtube;
- carrying out Live-broadcasts in social networks;
- commenting articles in social networks.

The conditions of Bounty campaign are published either in the main topic on BitcoinTalk or in the subsidiary with the prefix [Bounty]. I recommend creating a separate topic for Bounty, because otherwise in the main theme of the project, 80% will be bounty discussions.

This is an abstract example. You should determine your model based on the characteristics of your strategy. By the way, in well-developed technological projects, Pre-sale is more often private not public.

Executive Summary

In order to attract investment, you need to win the trust of the Blockchain community. It is important to publicly prove the viability of the project: to open the idea and business plan, to acquaint the community with the team and key figures of the project.

The basis of any ICO is a powerful, large-scale idea that can inspire thousands of people. The idea with a strong social component and an innovative business model.

In general, successful ICOs correspond to the following parameters:

1. The project should be about Blockchain or using Blockchain.
2. The project must have the potential of commercialization and scaling.
3. The project should surprise with the proposed approach to solving the problem.

Summary will best of all, describe your project since it reflects the basic parameters of your startup.

1. Project title.
2. Very short idea description.
3. Mission and Vision of your company.
4. Description of conception.
5. Product / Service - what you want to sell.
6. Business model of the project. What is your business?
7. Status of the project - at what stage it is, what is ready now, technical background (availability and quality of the prototype or source code).
8. About the team and yourself, the history of the project with an emphasis on expertise, business experience in the traditional market segment, in the Blockchain industry, the experience of block-development. The goal is to show that you are professionals in your niche.
9. Potential consumers and problems that the project solves.
10. Market and market niche - the volume of the

market, prospects and dynamics of the selected market niche for building a business.

11. The main competitors or existing companies on the market. The level of competitive pressures on the part of companies with similar business models from the traditional market segment and Blockchain-economy.

12. Comparison of your decision - why makes it radically better than competitors? Why should your consumers prefer your solution, not the decision of competitors?

13. Which platform is it implemented on Ethereum, Waves, NEM etc. or on his own?

14. The role of using Blockchain - use for a distributed ledger or to attract money?

15. How do you plan to use smart contracts? What are their key functions?

16. What is the purpose of the ICO, how much do you plan to collect? How much Soft Cap and Hard Cap? Why so much? What are you going to spend this money on, what to get as a result? How will the money be distributed?

17. What and in what time do you promise to do? The main points for the roadmap.

18. The role and function of the token. What kind of token, how many are going to be issued?

19. Conditions for buyers of the token, when, under what conditions you implement it.

20. How is your token more profitable than buying a crypto currency? Why is your token better than competitors' tokens? What are the closest successful analogues?

21. How will you ensure the liquidity of the token?

22. What are the bonuses, discounts and restrictions for token buyers?

23. How to buy a token for crypto currency? How to buy for Fiat money?

24. In which channels can you ask questions?

It will be a good idea to make a nice PDF presentation from this set of items.

Pre-announcement & Community involvement. Community management

The basis of each ICO is the adoption of a new project by the community. To collect the first user opinions, use the bitcoin-forum BitconTalk, the Bitcoin Forum section> Alternate cryptocurrencies> Announcements (Altcoins) and Reddit. You should Create a pre-announcement with the topic "Project name and basic idea", put the prefix [pre-ANN]. For example: [pre-ANN] EdFund - Crypto Fund for EdTech Startups.

Remember: when launching the main marketing campaign, change the prefix [pre-ANN] to [ANN] or [ICO] from the topic.

Pre-announcement is an announcement of the future project with the help of executive summary which is a small presentation about what we spoke above. After the Pre-announcement, you will receive the first feedback, having analysed which you will understand whether the project was able to interest investors or not.

After the release of the Pre-announcement there are often many questions about the business model of the project, about unaccounted risks, about suspicious aspects. Taking into account all incoming comments, your project receives a lot of useful material for corrections and finalization. Such process of feedback with subsequent improvements can be repeated several cycles, until there is no agreement between the founders, the community and potential investors.

After this stage, you develop the final business model of the project and write a detailed offer.

Now, the main thing: at the stage of interaction with the community, your project may end up. You can be charged with Scam, in bad faith or in using tokens without the need. In this case, you will be sent to seek investment elsewhere.

So, you should Pay close attention to the quality of the idea and the use of Blockchain in the Executive Summary.

WhitePaper Structure

White Paper is the main marketing document and Information Memorandum. Crypto investors decide on investing in your project relying on it. The document discloses data about the project and its objectives, the team of creators, mentors and partners involved in development. The main provisions for the issue and redemption of tokens are defined in it as well.

Therefore, it is important to allow you time for a good study of White Paper. Only a few will thoughtfully read your document, but these few will be crypto-enthusiasts with high authority in the community as well as with thousands of readers. They will easily raise you project or create problems for you.

If something in Whitepaper can be illustrated - do it. Investors will run through the text diagonally and focus on pictures, diagrams, charts, structures.

If you write Whitepaper yourself, give it to specialists: for $200- $500 per hour they will fix the problem areas.

It is necessary to divide information on White paper into sections. Widely WhitePaper describes:

- The essence of the project, prospects, Roadmap;
- The relevance of the project and the market in which it operates;
- The team;
- Project economics and token.

Typical structure of White Paper is the following:

- Background - how it all started.
- Introduction - the description of the market, the applicability of the Blockchain in it.
- Market Analysis which is a deep analysis of the market, market growth potential, existing competitors.
- Introduction to your Product, what kind of product, service or project do you offer.
- Product Specific Section. A detailed product description, graphics, tables, calculations.
- Technical Specifications. A detailed description of the technical aspects of the product.
- Use cases - product application practices.
- The pre-ICO (if pre-investment is carried out).
- Conditions for investors on the ICO, percentage of tokens which are going to be given to large investors, how many to the team and how much to retail.
- Roadmap of Development, what is done now, what is planned and what the deadlines are.
- Financial Projections, what will investment be spent on.
- Team - management, key employees and their experience, advisors.
- Conclusion which is the part where you draw the conclusions.

Writing White Paper is a sequence of steps:

- Forming the structure of the document of your ICO;
- Filling this structure with content;
- Primary design of the document;
- Discussion with the community. Perhaps you have several more times to finalize it and again discuss it with the community;
- Get the final draft and finalize the design;
- Translate into selected languages;
- Publish.

To achieve a high level of document quality, I recommend studying the development of at least a dozen of White Paper of such projects as Aeternity, Monetha, Bitcoin, Universa, etc.

Yellow Paper, One page & Light paper

Yellow paper is a technical specification document, which reflects all the technical aspects of the technology being developed. Yellow paper is a technical addition to White Paper and it is not a mandatory document for ICO. Nevertheless, if the project is conducted R&D after which there is a complex technological development, it is recommended to make a detailed Yellow paper.

Typical structure of Yellow Paper:

- Introduction;
- The Blockchain paradigm;
- Conventions;
- Blocks, states and transactions;
- Payment;
- Execution of Transactions;
- Creating a contract;
- Create a message;

- Execution Model;
- Completion of Block creation;
- Implementation of contracts;
- Future directions of development;
- Conclusion;
- References;
- Apps.

By analogy with writing White Paper, you will also need to discuss it with the community several times after writing the Yellow Paper.

Another non-mandatory ICO document is One page. One page is one-page PDF document briefly describing the project, its technology, advantages over competitors, key team members, economic model, token distribution and token sale Milestones. When creating One page, you need to pay special attention to its design and ergonomics.

Speaking of LightPaper, the principle of this document is about the same as that of One page, but the difference is that it is a bit more detailed and is created in contrast to One Page not in PDF but as part of the site in HTML.

In preparation for the ICO, there is no standardized approach and there are other numerous options for Papers such as Green Paper or even White Book. It is important that you are guided by one goal - to communicate the information about your startup to the consumer in a capacious and accessible way.

Stock Exchange Token Listings

Today there are hundreds of Cryptocurrency Trading Platforms and token exchanges on the market. These sites are independent and each has its own "set of preferences."

Therefore, in order to pass the listing procedure, it is required to conduct individual negotiations with their owners.

Each exchange defines a set of criteria that Digital Asses must meet for listing and bidding. The exchanges assess how much the token ccorresponds its reputation, mission and values , whether the token will be legalized in accordance with the US securities laws. But the main criterion is whether the demand for a token is high enough to extract profit from trading.

Some exchanges do not consider "investment tokens" - classified as securities or created solely for the collection of funds. At the same time, "useful tokens" should have a "clear and irrefutable reason" for existence. Some sites assess the level of security and liquidity of each asset, the structure and transparency of the ICO project.

The cost of placing a token on stock exchanges of the second echelon is from 1 to 50 Bitcoin.

The price in each case is calculated individually. For example, if you have your own Blockchain, then it is necessary to conduct technical work to integrate it into the work of the exchange, it will be much more expensive than adding a new ERC20 family token.

Exchanges of the first echelon possess a huge traffic of potential investors. But it's extremely difficult to get a little-known token on Bitfinex, GDAX or Poloniex. To begin with, negotiate with small exchanges, for example with https://etherdelta.com, understand their preferences and only then decide with which exchanges you will be partners with in the future. The more trading platforms after the ICO your token will trade on, the better its turnover will be. But evaluate the number of exchanges based on the budget possibilities. Try to make sure that your token is converted on the exchange site ShapeShift.io

Before contacting the management of the exchange, analyze their monthly traffic on SimilarWeb by estimating the monthly audience. Knowing the volume of the monthly audience, contact the site management and discuss the detail of listing.

WEBSITE, VIDEO AND PRESENTATION MATERIALS

Naming, Design & Brandbook

A great ship asks deep waters. Decide on the name. It should sound unique, innovative and promising. See how popular technological projects sound: Oculus, Xbox, Uber, Tesla. Learn the naming model of startups. The main thing that you need to remember is:

- The name should be short;
- It should be associated with what you are doing;
- The name should be written unambiguously;
- The domain of the site must be accessible.

Having defined the name, we create a logo. If you do not have a designer in the state, or a designer who for a bounty will develop you Corporate Identity, you can use the service of remote professionals Fiverr.com for graphics and any other tasks.

You also need a brand book. That is a document that creates an idea of your brand. It sets out a list of rules for the use of your trademark. In order to save money and time, do not develop a full brand book, limit what you need for ICO: logo design, business cards, some handouts and in your case maybe branded clothes, such as branded caps, polo or T-shirts.

In addition to the brand book, so that everything was in one style, you immediately need to take care of the design of the site, the design of social networks, presentations, White paper or other ICO documents. Make a single technical assignment for all the blocks of work and send it to the performers after having studied their portfolio.

Work on the website

The site is the central hub for interaction between the organising team, investors and the market during the ICO. ICO site will become the main source of information about your product, the landing point of advertising traffic, fundraising center, and at the same time the center for hacker attacks.

Before proceeding to any steps in the preparation of the site, you need to determine its main objectives, such as:
the description of your product,
demonstration of its advantages,
explanation of the market strategies of the future company,
the offer for investors,
the conversion of visitors into investors.

Working on the website includes the following stages:
1. Drawing up a technical task for the designer.
2. Purchase of domains in the .com, .io, etc. zones.

3. Buying a hosting or renting a server. To begin with, AWS from Amazon or Google will be suitable.

4. CDN connection.

5. Domain DNS binding to hosting.

6. Copyright. Preparation of texts for the website.

7. Design of pages. Selection of the best websites to use as examples.

8. Layout of page design in HTML and CSS. For this, a layout designer is needed.

9. Choosing or developing a CMS personal cabinet for investors who will buy tokens.

10. Creating a personal cabinet for investors.

11. Binding to smart contracts and developing a script for managing smart contracts for the distribution of tokens to investors in accordance with their contributions.

12. Binding of wallets for reception of cryptocurrencies (not always, though).

13. Connection to the layout of Google Analytics and other analytical systems.

14. Connecting the forms to CRM to manage ICO participants.

15. Testing the work of the website under a heavy load.

The structure of the Pre-ICO and ICO site can be one-page. To speed up the creation of the website, in the beginning you can use ready-made website design templates, for example on Themeforest only by modifying them to your needs. And do not forget to check them for viruses!

In developing the technical task for the designer, I recommend that in addition to the description, draw a sketch on A4 sheets and, together with the technical task file, send the photograph to the designer. It is important that when you make a technical assignment you send real texts that will be on the site, otherwise the change of texts may affect the layout.

Immediately take care of DDOs attacks, transferring the site's DNS to Cloudflare servers. Consult with CyberSecurity. ICO projects are often subjected to DDoS attacks during the ICO. As a result of such attacks, scammers imitate ICO sites with their phishing sites and steal money transferred by investors.

Translate the whole website. You can make it with the help of your team, hired translators for money or bounty rewards. Popular Languages for translation are: English, Chinese, Japanese, Korean, Russian, German, French.

The main functionality of the investor's personal cabinet:

- The Offer;
- Reception of crypto currency;
- The transfer of the released tokens to the wallet;
- Settings.

Additional functionality:

- Loading of identification documents;
- Additional two-factor protection;
- Different timers.

For development, I recommend that you contact experienced professionals, there are a lot of those, just look for them at BitcoinTalk.org.

Structure of the ICO site

The task of the website is to convey in detail the information about your idea and the structure of the forthcoming ICO. It is quite standard and consists of the following blocks:

- Main Video;
- Subscription Form;
- A noticeable button "invest";
- Countdown counter with the start date of the ICO. And after the beginning the counter with the end date of the ICO;
- Product Description. US Cases;
- Descriptions and conditions of ICO, Timeline;
- The form of buying a token;
- Examples of use;
- The Media that writes about you;
- Infographics;
- Roadmap: what and under which deadlines (break it down by quarters) ;
- Documents (White paper, Yellow paper) ;
- Additional videos or images;
- Team & Advisors: high-quality photos, short biographies, links to social networks. Media: photos with Vitalik Buterin, links to publications, videos of presentations and speeches;
- Partners;
- Scheme: how users can track the progress of the project;
- FAQ - collect all possible questions and publish them. As soon as new questions appear, enter them into the FAQ.

Surprisingly, only a few projects have a full-fledged section "Questions and Answers". The List of main issues is:

a. What is the economy of the token?
b. Why will the token be in demand?
c. Why do you need Blockchain?
d. How many tokens will be released?

e. Token distribution scheme

f. When will the token be on the exchange?

- Contacts, links to blogs and social networks and communication channels;
- Support.

Create Privacy Policy pages, Terms of Use & Policy of Use of Cookies files.

Video Production

Often, a 2-minute video allows you to understand the project better than 200 pages in White paper. Good visualization raises confidence at a subconscious level. Often entrepreneurs are trying to complicate the task of ordering costly animated videos. This is a mistake. Do not hide behind the animation. The task of the video is to explain how the project works, show the team, its intentions and proposals to investors.

Before producing a video, ask yourself a question - why do we need a video? Video should solve the problems and remove barriers.

Here are some typical ICO problems that can be easily solved through video.

1. No idea about the product. About 0.3% of the planet's population knows about the technology of Blockchain. How to describe a complex innovative product in plain language?
2. There is no confidence in the team. ICO is conducted by people who are not discusses in the media. How in a short time to tell about your experience, successes, intentions and energy?
3. There are no clear expectations after the ICO.

How to convince thousands of people from different countries that you are true to your idea and are confident in the plan of action? How to convey your faith in the final result and the desire to achieve the goal?

Here are a few examples that will help you develop the formats of your videos:

Interview with the team, where Live communication with key employees of the project is shown. Dialogues about the idea, about the experience, about the qualifications and the nearest plans for product development. Most relevant to show it first to Advisors and partners at the Pre sale stage.

The office, its atmosphere and working conditions are shown. The goal is to convey the mood of the team, drive, business approach and team cohesion. Show that you are 100 % passionate about the project. It is very important to show it on blogs during pre-Sale and ICO.

Pre-Roll Videos for Social Networks, where short cuts for emotional response in social networks are demonstrated. A special feature is the duplication of the audio message with graphic text.

Animation rollers. Visualization of complex ideas, voluminous structures and ambitious plans. Schematically explain the device technology, turn complex White Paper into a clear animation.

Promo Video. The key video is based on analyzing the target audience and adapting your idea to the target segments, speaking at conferences, online advertising, interaction with partners and the media.

As the stage of ICO preparation, you can create additional thematic videos, such as:

1. An overview video of the project.
2. «How it works» video.
3. The transformation of a complex White Paper into an understandable video.
4. Extended interview with the founders.
5. Suggestions of Advisors.
6. Shot-cuts of the opinions of industry experts.
7. An Inspiring movie: how the project changes the world.

But you do not have to do all these videos, the main thing is that a common set of video files will allow you to view your project in a complex way.

Project blog and social channels

The main rule of community management says: you should always stay in touch with your audience. Constantly show how you work, publish reports, shoot videos, write in social networks. It is better to do this 2 or 3 times a week.

Create social channels and publish Crossposting reports. Use all available channels of interaction with the audience:

• Blog on the site. You can use third-party platforms that provide external traffic, such as Medium, Golos, Steemit, Reddit.
• Rename the topic on the BitcoinTalk forum by changing the prefix to [ANN] or [ICO]. Create themes-copies in other language branches (now on the forum there are 19 language local branches). Put links from each channel to other channels.

- Mail Support.
- Reddit.
- Medium
- Telegram.
- Slack.
- Linkedin.
- If you have open source, then put a link to GitHub.
- If the resources of the team allow, then make a blog on YouTube.
-
  If you write in Chinese, then use WeChat and Weibo.

Facebook, Twitter & Instagram banned all ICO advertising. The next one who will do this is google (June 2018).

Email Marketing

The most important asset in the ICO is an investor. For him you are trying hard, he pays you money. All activities should be reduced to eliminating barriers and misunderstanding between you and an investor. For investors to invest, it is important to interact with them and communicate. There are not many channels where you can do this.

And the most effective and highly conversion channel of communication with the client base is Email. Email mailings are the core of any business. We're not talking about SPAM! Only those mailings on which the user expressed his consent and which he is waiting for are effective.

Traditionally, marketing is divided into technology of attracting customers and technology of customer retention. Email marketing is only about keeping investors' attention and working with their loyalty. The investor is hampered by the lack of trust in your team, lack of understanding of the technology's prospects, uncertainty about the potential of your token. Competently built mailing removes these objections and warms the potential investor to the ICO. The main mistake you can make while doing Email Marketing is getting into Spam. This will bring the end to all of your email marketing.

In order to avoid this, you should follow the following steps:

- Do not use someone else's e-mail database from your mail servers;
- Do not use your old database where a possible percentage of non-existent email accounts can be above 3%;
- Do not forget to ask specialists how to set up a mailing list so that it does not fall under spam filters. In particular, DKIM;
- Do not send empty mailings that do not contain useful information;
- Do not send out mailings more than once every 3 days. And it is better to send as often as often once a week.

How to make everything right:

- A Goal. Set a goal - for example using emails to remove fears of working with your startup.
- Scenarios. Create welcome-chains of letters that will consistently catch all new subscribers.
- The collection of the database: through the subscription forms, convert the visitors of your site to the subscriber. Offer them value: for example, an additional discount on a token, or a token as a gift, or research.

- The Segment the database. Send different emails for different segments of users.
- Tell interesting stories. The recipient must be engaged into the event processes.

To organize mailing, you need to perform 3 types of work:

- Make up the structure of the chain of letters;
- Copywriting conversations. Write shortly, beautifully. The subject of the letter is the most important detail for opening mail;
- Formalize mailing - do not forget about design.

What can be sent to subscribers:

- Weekly news - keep up to date with the project;
- Reminders of the investment date - month, week, day before the start;
- A reminder of the start of investment - five minutes before the start;
- Security notifications and links to step by step guidance.

LEGAL SCHEME AND LEGAL ASPECTS OF ICO

How to conduct an ICO and not break the law?

ICO is actually not a regulated area today. However, the events of recent months change the state of affairs in this industry. So, the authorities of China, Singapore and South Korea recently banned the ICO. True, China recently allowed again, but not yet definitively.

The United States Securities and Exchange Commission (SEC) said in July that many ICOs should be regulated by securities laws, and in September the SEC filed charges of fraud in the conduct of the ICO. In November the first collective lawsuit against the organizers of the ICO was filed in the United States. So far, SEC only warns about the risks of ICO, saying that certain tokens can be recognized as securities and their release must be accompanied by certain procedures and the admission to purchase only qualified investors.

Numerous signals make us think about the legalization and standardization of ICO processes.

In order not to violate the laws of different countries by accident, when conducting an ICO, you should worry about working out the legal part, paying attention to the following:

- The development of the general legal model of ICO,
- Choosing a legal scheme for tokens;
- Preparation of partnership documents for the company and partners;
- Preparation of an offer for investors with an indication of the entire ICO procedure (all possible situations where money will be spent, what kind of liability on the participants in case of non-compliance) ;
- Preparation of Escrow - a guarantor and execution of documents with it;
- Registration of a company, SUV or Holding;
- Registration of trademarks and intellectual property,
- Registration of a bank account;
- Accounting after ICO.

All these works should be conducted by professional lawyers with experience in Blockchain projects.

Criminal Liability

Some of the actions of the organizers of the ICO fall under criminal responsibility. The main source of danger is the lack of clear registration and the uncertainty of the status of the token.

In most jurisdictions, the statute of limitations for offenses related to money laundering and the financing of terrorism is 10 years. Among the main risks associated with raising funds during the ICO campaign, it is worth noting the following:

1. The risk of getting caught in taxarvation before the state of its tax residency.

2. The risk of violating the Foreign Account Tax Compliance Act (FATCA), which is the law on tax reporting on foreign accounts. Organizations that open accounts for US citizens are required to report to US authorities.
3. The risk of violating the rules of the jurisdiction of the legal entity that sells tokens, such as:
   - incorrect registration of the ICO campaign at registration;
   - incorrect accounting reporting;
   - incorrect registration of transfer of rights to tokens from one person to another, violation of tax legislation.

Hire an international Blockchain lawyer. Do not save on these expenses, it is better to overpay a competent lawyer than bear the risk of criminal prosecution. Most of the practicing lawyers are not competent in the Blockchain sphere. A lawyer must officially be responsible for his expertise. Be sure to clarify from a lawyer, citizens of which countries at the time of the ICO you can not sell tokens to. For example, for Crowd sale with the citizens of Singapore, you can get criminal punishment of up to 12 years of imprisonment!

In addition to citizens of the United States, Singapore, China, you should also be curious with citizens of countries controlled by the United States, as well as with citizens of South Korea, China, Virgin Islands of the United States, etc. Probably in the near future this list will expand to other countries such as Great Britain, Russia and some EU countries.

Know Your Customer (KYC)

An important aspect in the ICO process is an identification of crypto-investors, or as they say in financial institutions - know your customer or KYC.

It's no secret that crypto-currency speculative investments are almost synonymous with anonymity today. Many ICO investors do not want to pay taxes on earned tokens, so they do not want to disclose their identity.

For the ICO project, the forced identification and installation of the counterpart's personality can reduce the conversion of investments by several times.

But there are 4 factors why it is desirable to identify investors:

1. Conducting KYC in relation to potential buyers of tokens may be required by the legislation of the country of incorporation of the company - the issuer of the token.
2. Conducting KYC is necessary in order to protect the issuer as much as possible from the risks of violation of the legislation of some countries on securities, which limit the turnover of virtual currencies.

3. Carrying out identification of buyers of tokens will simplify the further conversion of crypto currency into Fiat money.

4. If you do not identify users, you will not be able to conduct an IPO of your company.
5. If you do not identify your crypto-investors, when you credit funds to a bank account, there is a high risk to get under bank sanctions in the field of countering money laundering through criminal means.

Tax aspects of ICO

When paying income tax on individuals it is important to consider the compatibility of your tax residency and the jurisdiction of the ICO campaign. Properly organized ICO should not be taxable at the venue.

It is important to find such jurisdiction in which the revenue of the issuing company of the tokens will not be subject to local corporate taxes.

The receipt of taxable profits when placing tokens depends on the structure of the token and the commitments made by the ICO's organizers. The task of lawyers is to organize the proper structuring of the ICO and to offer the lowest tax burden for the issuer.

I insist that in legal and fiscal aspects you attract experienced professionals!

What is a Token from a Legal Point of View?

From a legal point of view, tokens can take different forms:
1. Asset or product.
2. Payment means (in Australia and Japan).
3. Foreign currency (in Argentina).
4. Services.
5. A record in the registry (a draft of an undisclosed law in Delaware).
6. Bonus points.

At the legislative level, the concept of a token is defined in Germany and Japan. In most cases, the definition of a token is not given directly by law, but is given by the instructions of the tax authorities and by laws that have the force of law in the courts of many countries, for example, in Singapore and Israel.

After you have determined what is a token, you need to

understand what legal action you will take when collecting funds through the ICO:

- crowning vesting company;
- crowdfunding company;
- provision of services;
- barter exchange;
- collecting donations;
- registration in the register with charging;
- distribution of bonus points.

In the legal structuring of the token for the EU, the US and China, individual legal models are being worked out.

Checking Token on Securities

In order to determine whether the token refers to Securities, there are 3 tests.

1. Howey Test is the main test that determines whether the token is securities or not.
2. Risk Capital Test.
3. Family Resemblance test.

If your token meets the definition of Securities, and you are going to conduct ICO in US-controlled jurisdictions, then prepare to a more complicated preparation of ICO, it will lengthen in time, will cost more and involve highly qualified investors.

Preparation of the Offer

After the company received confirmation of interest in the project from Blockchain Community, developed a financial and business model of the project, lawyers write a detailed offer for investors.

An offer means being ready to make a deal in which significant terms and conditions of the contract are set out, addressed to a certain person, to a limited or unrestricted circle of persons.

An offer is made on behalf of a registered company or on behalf of the founder of the company that launches the ICO. The offer is a legal document drawn up by lawyers. The offer specifies the detailed terms of the contract with the crypto-investors and your obligations to them.

The offer describes all the points of the project, talking about:

- type of financial instrument token,
- all rights of the token,
- the minimum required and desired amount of investment,
- the terms of project implementation,
- the type of financial instrument used (token, crypto currency, coin),
- terms of withdrawal to the stock exchange.

Often, those who are in Singapore, the United States, Puerto Rico, the Virgin Islands of the United States and other dependent territories of the United States are excluded from the offer.

Blockchain lawyers usually have basic types of offer templates and finalizing an offer for you should not take more than a few days.

Risks & Due Diligence

From the perspective of investors, the main risk with ICO is the loss of their investments due to fraud of the organizers. There are a lot of scammers on the ICO market.

Before the ICO on the Internet there was a huge number of groups that organized the pyramid scheme. Having seen the model and the ICO niche, many of them switched to it. So recently, the Confido project disappeared from the radar, which raised $ 374,000 on the ICO.

Given that ICO is almost not regulated thing, scammers have a legal opportunity under the guise of steep mega-projects to take money from inexperienced crypto-investors. The lack of legal regulation of this procedure does not allow investors to protect their rights in the event of theft of funds invested into ICO. This makes investors extremely cautious when choosing ICO for investment. The problem is aggravated also by a multitude of low-quality ICOs, and ICOs after which they noted the misuse of collected funds. At the heart of these problems is the lack of legal regulation of the Initial Offering procedure in many countries of the world. This is the main ICO risk for both organizers and investors. But beyond this there are a number of other risks for entrepreneurs.

I distinguish 5 types of risks for the organizers of ICO:

1. Organizational risks. This type of risk will not allow you to achieve the planned level of funding due to poor preparation for the ICO process. The reasons may be: inadequate elaboration of the concept, weak marketing campaign, opacity of the team or unviable plans for the development of the project.
2. Legal risks. The most dangerous of risks. You can conduct a successful ICO, reach a CAP, but later endure litigation or criminal prosecution. These risks include: denial of opening a bank account, recognition of a token by a monetary surrogate, prohibition of ICO or a resolution on the return of

funds to investors.

3. Technical risks: unfinished smart contracts can allow attackers to steal your assets, as was the case with DAO. At the most critical moment, your server can not withstand the loads from a large influx of users and the site will be unavailable. Open source code can fail.

4. Fraudulent risks. Conducting a successful ICO campaign, your project can be exposed to Scam impacts as hacking the server and substituting the wallet address for fraudulent, hacks of your wallets and stealing all collected funds, DDoS attacks, Phishing, etc.

5. Market risks. This may be the volatility of the crypto currency market, because in 2-8 weeks of your ICO, popular crypto-currencies can change their value relatively to the dollar. Another risk may be a change in the regulator in the country of incorporation of the company, as a result of which your ICO may be outside the legal field and lead to a depreciation of the token.

The situation that developed around the crypto currency, resembles the times of the Ponzi schemes. In order to avoid risks and be prepared for Due Diligence, a diligent ICO project should:

- Prove to potential investors the validity of the ICO and the need to issue its own crypto currency;
- Disclose plans for the development of the project and conduct an open dialogue with potential investors,
- Spread and constantly update the Open Source;
- Provide the ability of Mining of Coins to involve new users and provide the network with the necessary resources for processing transactions;
- Go to the ICO with a clear understanding of the size of the amount involved;

- The founding team must own between 10% and 50% of all tokens and should not exchange them for several years.

According to experts, the majority of existing projects in 2018 may not fulfil the obligations imposed or even be fraudulent. This is because it's easier to invest, and people invest their money without evaluating the company, without spending Due Diligence.

Due Diligence is used to conduct an in-depth analysis of the investment object. In the case of the critical economy and ICO projects, Due Diligence is superficial, which often leads to investing in projects beyond which there is no real business.

To protect depositors, by analogy with the traditional financial market, new players appear on crypto market - rating agencies. Such agencies conduct independent Due Diligence, analyze all information about the company and publish the results of their research in the form of an independent rating review, indicating the strengths and weaknesses of the projects.

If you want to convince potential ICO investors in the reliability of your intentions, it is recommended to involve rating agencies with a well-deserved reputation, such as for example ICORating. ICORating conducts research of all aspects of the project that are behind a specific crypto currency financial instrument. The company analyses the investment risks of the upcoming ICO in the following areas:

- Relevance, strengths and weaknesses of the business model;
- Prospectivity and dynamics of the development of the market niche;

- Experience and reputation of the team;
- The level of competitive pressure from companies which have similar business models
- Technical background (availability and quality of the prototype or source code);
- Analysis of feedback from the community, etc.

Having conducted Due Diligence, investors in free access will be able to see how risky this or that investment is.

Another way to increase investor confidence can be to involve the third party in the form of arbitrators who are trusted by investors, acting as an intermediary between them and projects.

The most common way today is to form a legal entity and limit the project team to the expense of funds received through the ICO.

Escrow, Anti-Scam & Multi-sig Wallets

If there are no well-deserved celebrities among your team, try to demonstrate your intention to keep their means with the help of Escrow. Cryptographic Escrow is carried out with the help of Multi-sig wallets and independent escrow agents. This means that the company collects money not directly, but with the involvement of third parties who act as depositary agents.

MultiSig-wallet does not allow to spend money without a one-time consent of all signature holders. Access to the MultiSig-wallet is available only to deposit agents, which, in turn, provide additional protection. Thus, the company can not independently spend the collected money without the digital signature of the agent.

In this case, the ICO can be compared to a venture capital investment scheme, when financing is broken down into rounds, which is carried out by the depositary agent holding the funds. He compares the compliance of the development of the start-up with the declared in the roadmap and confirms the payments. The duties of a deposit agent include checking the fulfillment of the terms of the offer by the startup team, meeting deadlines and obligations to investors. Only if the stated conditions are met, the company gets access to the following payments from the Multi-sig wallet.

In practice, it looks like this - the company collects $1 million. The business model implementation plan is divided into 10 periods. The first $100 thousand company receives from the Multi-sig wallet immediately after the end of the collection of money. The longer the deposit agent oversees the fulfillment of the stated conditions, the integrity of the issuing company, the compliance with the terms and, in the case of the successful completion of the first phase of the plan, issues the next part of the amount. If the company does not fulfil its obligations, the money remains frozen in the wallet before fulfilling obligations or returned to investors.

It is important that the role of Escrow agent is carried our by a reliable person (or group of people), because the responsibility for the money is borne by the company, not by the Escrow agent.

Choice of jurisdiction and company registration for ICO

The first legal question asked by the organizers of the ICO is the jurisdiction of which country to choose for the company?

The choice of jurisdiction is the definition of a country whose legislation will apply:

- To individuals - organizers of the ICO;
- To actions of the legal entity;
- To actions of buyers of tokens.

For this reason countries with a more favorable legislative and tax regime are selected for the ICO. The choice of a jurisdiction is not just tax and legislative preferences. Banks and financial regulators significantly complicate this procedure because of their different positions in relation to the ICO.

When choosing a jurisdiction, it is necessary to assess not only legal aspects, but also political, economic, fiscal and social ones. Before proceeding with the registration of a company, it is necessary to work out a model for the withdrawal of crypto currency in fiat money. Ask yourself the question: do you need fiat money, or can you develop your project solely for crypto-currencies? If the money is still needed, then the collected crypto currency can be sold through the exchange. Not how to export this crypto currency from the exchange? In the legal legal field, the company must have a bank account - this is the weak link of any ICO. Which bank will open an account for a company that receives income from nothing. In this case, the cryptocurrency is not considered by the financial authorities as a commodity and only a few banks will be ready to work with such ICO company.

So once you decide on the jurisdiction before the company is re-registered, you need to negotiate with the bank so that it confirms the agreement to work with your ICO in the jurisdiction you choose.

Organizational structure

We will consider three structures: holding, special purpose vehicle company (SPV) and the Fund.

The parent holding company for ICO can be registered in different jurisdictions, except the Isle of Man. When analyzing the holding jurisdictions of registered companies conducted by ICO, TOP-3, these are: the USA, Switzerland and Singapore. Gibraltar is the leader in the amount of funds raised among the holdings, where the largest amounts were collected from the TOP-30 largest ICO.

The model of working with SPV is roughly the following: the holding company registers the temporary SPV that holds the ICO. All intellectual rights are registered with the holding company this is necessary to protect against risks. SPV for ICO is most often an offshore company registered in Gibraltar, BVI, Isle of Man or in other offshore jurisdictions where ICO is not banned and with which white banks operate.

Why is it a good idea to register SPV? One of the reasons is that if there are any claims to the ICO, the claims will follow to SPV, in the extreme case it can be liquidated, but the project itself will continue to exist, because the copyrights are with the parent company.

ICO for the Fund

For offshore ICO funds, for example, invested in Blockchain projects, the jurisdictions of Cyprus, the Cayman Islands and Bermuda are traditionally suitable.

Despite their island affiliation, these jurisdictions are considered to be practically white. The Caymans and Bermuda recently figured in the leaked archives of the

"Paradise Papers", where it became clear that even the Queen of Great Britain holds her capital there! But these jurisdictions function in the US legal field. This is good for protecting your investments, but complicates the operational processes for investing in ICO.

ICO in Hong Kong

Today, there are jurisdictions both with a favorable environment and the jurisdictions in which ICO conduct is either unprofitable or prohibited.

After the ban on the conduct of ICO by China's regulators, the Hong Kong Futures and Securities Commission has subsequently published a statement regarding the conduct of the ICO. It turned out that a token in Hong Kong can be recognised as an investment instrument if it has the following properties:

- if the token provides property or corporate rights;
- if by its nature a token is a unit in a collective investment scheme;
- if the token is a debt instrument.

Any operation with such a token will be a part of the regulated financial activity. When carrying out such operations, the company must have the necessary permits and licenses.

ICO in Canada

The financial regulator of Canada published a statement regarding the conduct of ICO in the territory of its jurisdiction. The statement indicates that under certain actual circumstances, the application of securities legislation may be applied to the ICO. Also, factors were mentioned that indicate that the token is an investment instrument. In addition, the Financial Controller of Canada has requested exchanges for crypto currency to properly maintain accountability, follow all AML procedures and comply with identification requirements. Therefore, Canada is a good jurisdiction for long-term projects with a financial core inside.

ICO in Singapore

The financial regulators of Singapore published the main risks that investors should take into account when participating in the ICO.

Based on the risk map, the ICO project has a high degree of risk if:

- There is no incorporation in the territory of Singapore;
- Has no guarantees of liquidity of tokens in the secondary market;
- Promises extremely high token yield;
- Does not have at all, or has unverified information about sellers of tokens and / or issuers.

Singapore's regulator called on investors to take all risks into account and try to minimize them. For companies this means increased interest from regulators, complicated registration and possible taxation in Singapore.

ICO in the USA

The United States Securities and Exchange Commission, the SEC outlined the position regarding crypto-economics and the sale of tokens and began to fight against companies that do not comply with the law. According to the SEC, in the markets of crypto currency risks of manipulation and widespread practices of "pump-

and-dump", which are banned in the US, are increased.

What does it mean? Now, crypto-economists selling tokens that fall under the definition of securities must comply with the requirements of the US securities legislation:

- Such tokens must be registered with the SEC or subject to the exceptions specified in the law;
- Persons carrying out operations for the exchange of tokens must register as exchanges for the exchange of securities or fall under the exceptions specified in the law.

If the factor of passing the procedures of the SEC does not scare you, then the US, Delaware is one of the most promising and respectable jurisdictions. Conducting ICO in the United States is beneficial, primarily for residents of this jurisdiction.

ICO in Malaysia

The ICO in Malaysia is closely monitored by the Securities Commission Malaysia (SCM).

SCM claims that participation in the ICO is connected with the risks of lack of legal protection, and the risks of a sharp fluctuation in the price of the token on the secondary market. Nevertheless, Securities Commission Malaysia has a very low-key position on the ICO and does not consider it a source of massive abuse, which allows considering this jurisdiction as one of the potential for ICO in Asia.

ICO in Israel

The Israel Securities Authority (ISA) formed a committee whose main task is to develop rules for the regulation of the ICO. The regulator took a clear position and advocates the introduction of mechanisms that will help protect investors, as well as the introduction of ICO in the legal field. Most likely, in the near future Israel will set a number of rules and standards for ICO campaigns.

ICO in Liechtenstein

Quite recently, Liechtenstein, where the financial regulator of the Financial Market Authority Liechtenstein (FMA) has approved the conduct of a number of ICOs in the jurisdiction, has joined these countries authorizing the ICO. Along with Switzerland, Liechtenstein is one of the most respectable jurisdictions for doing business. But what can cause complications is the process of registration of the company, because in each case, the decision will be made by the Financial Market Authority Liechtenstein (FMA) individually.

ICO in Switzerland & Crypto Valley

At the end of 2016, the development of rules that would allow raising up to 1 million Swiss francs within the ICO without obligation to report to the securities market regulator was announced in Switzerland. Such an easing can attract companies into this jurisdiction that are relevant to the requirement, inn fact 1 million CHF is slightly more than 1 million USD, the amount is quite sufficient for the development of a technological start-up.

But in spite of this easing, business in Switzerland requires strong legal support because there is very strong legal framework in the country. Swiss regulators are quite loyal to crypto-currencies, but in its jurisdiction there are many rules and features of doing business.

Canton of Zug is Optimal for the ICO, this is the Swiss Crypto Valley - an area with dozens of startups in the area of Cryptocurrency & Blockchain. Among the founders of the Crypto Valley Association are Thomson Reuters, PwC, Luxoft, Bitcoin Suisse which is quite a decent company for a good start. There is also the Ethereum Foundation registration office we visited last winter.

Ban on ICO in China

China, which has recently launched 10 internal ICO per day, is no longer a jurisdiction for ICO. ICO in China is outlawed. This was announced by 7 Chinese regulators. The ban came after the Central Bank of the Republic of China discovered a huge number of cases of fraudulent collection of funds from the population through the ICO. The bank decided to return the funds raised during the ICO to investors. Also, all credit institutions received a ban on cooperation with companies conducting ICO. The ban also applies to crypto-exchanges - now you can not place your tokens there.

For companies only going to conduct an ICO it is recommended:

- to make it impossible to sell tokens to the citizens of the PRC (the People's Republic of China) and on the territory of the PRC;
- to make it technically impossible on the territory of the PRC to sell tokens to Chinese citizens and on the territory of the PRC.

In addition, it is necessary to limit advertising demonstration and marketing activities for the territory of China.

ICO in Japan

In Japan, crypto currency is a legal means of payment. But Japan's tax system is "pretty tough" and work with Japanese residents is complicated by a number of barriers: linguistic, legal, and economic.

Currently, the Japanese Council on Audit Standards plans to prepare for a set of conditions for the circulation of crypto currency. Also, Japan's Financial Services Agency (FSA) has approved 11 companies as operators of cryptocurrency exchanges.

In the country, the rules for the circulation of the Crypto-currency are formalized, including those relating to its mining, trade and possibly the conduct of the ICO. In addition, there are guidelines for Japan's Ministry of Economy, Trade and Industry (METI) on the evaluation of various Blockchain projects.

The country is loyal to everything that concerns crypto-currencies, but at the same time due to regional specifics one can experience some difficulties in conducting ICO.

Selecting a bank and registering a bank account

Most of these services, such as office rent, payment of communication and electricity can not be paid by bitcoins or Ethers. Therefore, as far as the founders of the block-start-ups do not want to be independent of states and jurisdictions, sooner or later the funds received during the ICO campaign will have to be legalized and withdrawn in a fiat currency to a bank account.

You can register a company in any jurisdiction, or

structure a holding of any complexity, but without the consent of the bank to work with a crypto-currency company, whole legal scheme will not cost anything. Therefore, the bank must be selected before the start of the ICO, and before the company is registered. Before you spend money on the legal scheme, you must agree with the bank on cooperation.

I must say, this is the most difficult step in the ICO. No bank opens an account, nominated in the crypto currency. And only rare banks open accounts for companies associated with crypto-currencies. For example, out of 300 banks located in 43 jurisdictions that our partners interviewed, only 11 banks expressed their readiness to individually review projects related to the ICO. One of these banks Fidor Bank (www.fidor.de) is a German digital-only challenger bank that develops banking services. A bank has a good reliability rating B + by S & P. The peculiarity of the bank is that it is necessary to show a presence in Germany - either a legal entity or a representative office.

Singapore's OCBC Bank is also ready to consider opening accounts for companies working with crypto-currencies. The problem is that when a Singapore company receives money on an account, this creates a risk of tax consequences in Singapore and thus your ICO will be more expensive. In addition, you will need to agree on operational activities with the Monetary Authority of Singapore (MAS), and this will lead to forced work with exchanges licensed by MAS.

If you are an active entrepreneur, first of all talk to your current bank. It's also worth trying to chat with UBS, Falcon Bank and other private banks.

In Japan, Bank of Yokohama and SBI Sumishin Net Bank work with blockchain projects. But as I have said above, the problem of the language barrier is acute in

Japanese companies.

Offshore banks with a low reliability rating are not recommended. It may happen that after you transfer your funds from exchanges to bank accounts, you will find out that your bank has ceased to exist. This unfortunately happens.

An alternative solution is to search for service providers - specialized financial organizations that provide intermediary functions related to the transfer of monetary funds. In fact, these are payment systems that become intermediary between you and the bank. But in this case you are not protected as a bank depositor. Such companies do not have a reliability rating, if something happens to them, then you will not receive compensation provided in case of bankruptcy of the bank.

You need to be absolutely transparent with the bank. The dialogue should be structured roughly as follows: we have a transparent business, and we want to receive revenue from the sale of the crypto currency that was earned as a result of the ICO.

Do not withhold the belonging to the crypt world - in case of deception, you can be blocked by the account until the circumstances become clear.

PROMOTION OF ICO: MARKETING AND PR CAMPAIGN

ICO Target Audience

Before proceeding to the marketing discussion, check that the start dates for your ICO do not fall on dead periods (for example, Christmas, New Year or high summer season).

Target Audience is the audience, which in the first place, is directed to the marketing promotion of the ICO campaign.

In fact, you should work with 3 types of audiences:

1. Blockchain-evangelists. They Respond to technology, designed to make a breakthrough in the development of Blockchain projects. If they appreciate your idea,

your ICO will be successful.

2. Crypto-speculators and holders of crypto-currency. Speculators are short-term investors, they enter the ICO at the most profitable stages and sell the token among the first at the time of listing.

   Long-term investors will acquire a token in the first days of the campaign and will hold it for a long time in anticipation of multiple growth.

3. Potential users of your technology. Those who will use your product and for this buy a token that is integrated into it. This is the most loyal and valuable audience that has decided to become a part of your community.

Depending on your industry and the niche of your project, select additional, more specific segments of the target audience and continue working with them.

Target Audience can be found on specialized resources. The task of your marketing directors is to organize the promotion of ICO so that from all the traffic channel you allocate your target segments.

Media plan. 23 channels for a successful ICO Promotion

ICO provides tremendous opportunities for advancement. To conduct an ICO, you can use all available tools: media, conferences, targeted advertising. The larger the initial ICO budget, the more likely is a successful funding.

But in order to monitor such a large-scale promo campaign and manage it, you need to develop a Media Plan. A simplified model of Media Plan for ICO can display only advertising activities and incoming traffic channels.

ICO-trackers. The first channel, which gives not only the targeted traffic but also reflects your reputation is ICO-trackers. Trackers study your project, and if it does not look like SCAM, place it on their list. Some sites can ask for money for placement or for a detailed review , that can be from $500 to $3000.

PR activity. The more Blockchain & Cryptocurrency sites, such as coindesk.com write about your ICO, the better. Surely, it is not for free. Some sites charge several tens of thousands of dollars for placing information about the ICO. A list of such sites should be identified in advance, and then you should contact their representatives to discuss the conditions of placement. Find an experienced PR-manager. Before deciding to pay or not to pay, analyze the traffic of sites using Similarweb.

Tech blogs. I remember my delight, after the first article about our team in Techcrunch. In addition to enthusiasm, an article from this Tech blog gave us about thousand transitions a day during the week. Tech blogs are a market indicator. If you are written about in WIRED, Cnet, Mashable and Gizmodo - all other media will understand that you invented something really outstanding.

Forums and blogs. BitcoinTalk is one of the most important sources of thematic traffic. Make sure to give it special attention. But have a look at the other forums from the above links and Goggle, as well.

Reddit promotion. Can you work with Reddit? If not, then attract someone who can. Ignoring the site of this level is simply impossible.

Medium and Steemit promotion. According to the

Similarweb service, the monthly average audience is 126 million people. Write in blogs, write, and write again.

Facebook advertising. High-precision, but at the same time high-cost type of traffic attraction. Give this block to a specialist, setting him the task of identifying potential ICO investors. After the ban to advertise ICO you can only have your ICO page and Group in the Facebook and conduct on it organic traffic, without advertising tools.

Promotion in LinkedIn. Act the same as with Facebook.

Advertising in Instagram. The basis of advancement in Instagram is in visual emotionality. There are products that can cause emotional reactions. If your product is not like this, do not waste money. After the ban to advertise ICO you can only have your account in the Instagram and conduct on it organic traffic, without advertising tools.

Promotion of YouTube channel. I do not recommend paying for paid presentations of your videos. But the more videos you watch and comment, the higher and more popular they will become. Think about which groups and which sites to host video for the most coverage.

Streaming / Live video on Facebook, Instagram. Broadcast all your offline activities here, meet ups & workshops. Attract the bounty community.

SEO site. I'm not sure that in 4-5 months of ICO preparation you will have time to make significant progress on your keywords, but at least by the name of your product and its ICO you definitely have to be in the first place in all search engines. Sometimes it takes 3 months.

Contextual advertising Google, Bing, Yahoo.

Expensive clicks, large traffic and small conversion. But it's worth trying, what if your segment has a higher conversion?

Email-mailing. Keep your customers in the forefront of events, but do not overdo it. Your task is to bring them at the right time to your website.

Chat bots. The popularity of Facebook Messenger, Viber & Telegram forces marketers to conduct additional activities in these messengers. To interact with audiences, special channels are created, for which you can create specialised bots using the API. This is at the same time both convenient and not, since many users do not like when intrusive marketers invade their space. The use of bots should to be extremely selective in the messages sent to users. Get an audience and interact with it. It's comfortable.

Business sites. Usually Forbes writes about those who have already achieved much. But if your business has a really breakthrough idea, sites like Businessinsider, Bloomberg and WSJ can raise the reputation of your product to the highest level.

Financial sites. Set the task for your PR specialists to work out everything that is connected with finances and investments. Especially if you have a model how you can involve FIAT Investors into ICO.

Conference. They do not lead directly to the purchase of the token. But they can be useful in large numbers, if instead of your team you are constantly promoted at them by your advisors or motivated bounty ambassadors.

Meet ups and Workshops. Organize event activities with your community, broadcast them all to streaming channels. Inform the audience in advance. But remember - the result of any event should be some kind of action. For example, a subscription to the newsletter on your website.

Startup-competitions and ICO competitions. Direct traffic will most likely not be given, but they can help increase the recognition of your company.

Blockchain-enthusiasts. In the world of Blockchain expertise and authority play a significant role. Bring the leading Blockchain guru to your project. If they approve your company, a big Blockchain community will come to you.

Crypto-currency investment funds. Such funds as Draper Associates and Blockchain Capital specialism in crypto-currency investments. Offer your project to them, but be prepared for a deep Due Diligence.

Other channels of communication. Team Slack can be available to your potential investors. Similarly, if you decide to work with a Chinese audience, use WeChat.

Also you should know that after 06/18 Google will ban ICO advertisement.

Content Marketing & Writing Articles

Content-marketing is a separate category of marketing, the arsenal of which should be owned by your PR-manager. Content marketing includes:

1. Creating a structure of the content plan.
2. Preparation of graphic materials.
3. Writing articles.
4. Develop an interview.
5. Creating Content for Social Networks.

6. Creation of a list of advertising platforms and interaction with editors.

Further, the content is developed and consequently, in accordance with the plan, is placed in all the channels of promotion.

If, for some reason, you do not have a specialist, who will develop a content strategy for promoting your ICO, here are the minimum set of articles that your team must write on their own:

1. How was the idea of the product born?
2. What is the project changing in the world?
3. The Description of the project.
4. Interview with the creator.
5. Article with sharing experience and knowledge.

In all articles, blogs and social channels, write about metrics: publish data on the number of email subscribers, members of social channels, analysts' forecasts about the high demand for your tokens. Describe bonuses and discounts to the first investors.

Targeted Blockchain Traffic

The first thing you need to do is to analyze ICO traffic of your competitors' websites, those which are closest to your topic. This can be done through the SimilarWeb service. There you can find out from what sources the transitions to the sites you are interested in are carried out.

Also, there are a number of exchanges that sell Cryptocurrency traffic.

Run other advertising as well. Use any traffic sources that you can work with. Your main task is to make the tokens sold on the first day.

TECHNICAL DEVELOPMENT FOR ICO

7 Blockchain Infrastructure Providers & Platforms for the Tokens Issue

Even if you are developing your own Blockchain, it is more rational to conduct ICO on existing Blockchain-platforms, where tokens are issued, and investors buy them for popular crypto-currencies.

Ethereum

The most popular platform for Blockchain-start-ups and the release of tokens is now Ethereum with its own crypto-currency Ether (ETH). The Ethereum platform hosts most of the ICO. Ethereum is created for projects that work with smart-contracts and with ERC-20 tokens.

Implementation on Ethereum involves programming the token and its functionality manually. This is quite simplified, and there are many examples of code implementation on the network.

At the same time, there are platforms that make it

possible to realise the necessary functions much more simply because they offer users already ready-made technical solutions.

NEM

NEM is a Japanese platform. On the basis of NEM, the issue of the DIMCOIN coin was recently held, the ICO of which raised $ 10 million. NEM uses its own blockchain technology with the Proof-of-Importance algorithm.

Waves

The Waves platform was developed by the Russian team, which collected $ 18 million at ICO. Waves launched ICO Primalbase, which collected $ 5 million dollars in less than a day. In addition, Waves operates as a decentralized exchange with a trading volume of about 600 thousand dollars a day. The platform is quite promising, but in my opinion today is still quite raw.

NXT / Ardor

The NXT platform was created by an anonymous author in 2013. Today, the control over NXT belongs to the non-profit organization NXT Foundation. In addition to releasing tokens, the platform operates as a decentralized exchange with a daily turnover of about $ 40,000 per day.

Counterparty

Since 2014 the Counterparty platform has become a platform for many ICOs, including the widely known Storj data storage. The daily turnover of the decentralized exchange is about $20k. Counterpart works on the blockchain bitcoin, so every transaction requires in addition to the internal currency of the platform, XCP, and also bitcoins to pay for costs.

BitShares

BitShares is a decentralized exchange with a daily turnover of more than $ 1 million, as well as a platform for creating smart contracts on the Proof-of-Stake protocol. For all operations of buying, selling and issuing tokens, fees are charged in the platform's own currency, BTS.

Lisk

Lisk is a Blockchain Application Platform Used to create applications and generate Digital Assets Javascript which is one of the most popular languages that most programmers and developers own.

Despite the abundance of new and emerging exotic platforms, it is easier to launch ICO with Ethereum, which already has its own ecosystem of developers and token holders.

Blockchain Programming Languages. Solidity. Hiring programmers and developers

If you create your Blockchain, you need at least three types of specialists:

Blockchain engineer who is a core-developer with serious experience in system programming in C / C ++ or Java.

Blockchain developer is a developer with very good experience in the same programming languages.

Smart contracts developer. Professionals with experience in developing Web applications (for example, in JavaScript or Python) will be suitable here.

If you are not going to develop your Blockchain, and expect to use third-party Blockchain platforms, I recommend you to consider Ethereum. Ethereum is convenient for writing smart contracts and issuing tokens, there are enough specialists on the market who have mastered it.

You will need Solidity developers. Solidity is a contract-oriented language for implementing smart contracts.

The syntax is similar to that of the Ethereum Virtual Machine.

Because of the high demand for the programming of smart contracts, the cost of Blockchain programmers is several times higher than the cost of programmers not related to Blockchain. But, thanks to the similarity with Javascript, in order to save some money, you can search for experienced programmers in Javascript.

For simple Smart Contracts, you can search for developers at Fiverr.com or on Bitcoin & Blockchain-oriented forums. I often meet programmers on Mitapah and Hakaton. Also, in social networks and on the headhunting websites.

Issue of tokens and development of Smart contracts for Ethereum

Ethereum tokens are also described on the official Ethereum website.

Currently, the standard for the token is ERC20.

Issue of tokens on the ICO, depending on the settings of Smart Contracts can be carried out in two ways:

- immediately after the transfer of the crypto currency to the Smart Contract wallet in proportion to the amount of fees;
- after collecting all the necessary amount of CAP.

In the second case, tokens are distributed among investors in proportion to the size of the amount collected.

How does the process of issue of tokens look like?

The code for Smart Contract is written, it describes the rules for the appearance of new tokens, and deploy on Blockchain. After the release of the tokens, any number of them can be sent to any wallet in the Blockchain. Before the start of Crowd sale on the website, you specify the addresses of your wallets (or wallets of your Smart Contracts) for collecting crypto currency. This can be Bitcoin, Ethereum and other currencies. You collect money for these wallets.

If you are an experienced developer, then to create a token you can use Geth which is a convenient command-line interface for working with Node of Ethereum.

But for beginners, generating tokens and creating smart contracts is more convenient to make from:
- the official Ethereum of the Mist wallet, where the Smart-Contract will be directly written and launched;
- the browser wallet Metamask.

Metamask is more convenient for creating first tokens and smart contracts in test networks. The real Crowd sale should be run on the Mist.

In order not to pay real Ethrer for the execution of contracts in Blockchain Etherium, to test smart contacts we will create a test network. Download the wallet, wait until all the blocks are updated. It may take several hours, the status of the update is displayed in the lower left corner. Switch to the testnet: go in the menu develop, choose network, choose Ropsten or Rinkeby test network. Again, you will need some time to synchronise the entire Blockchain.

To download our contract to the network, we need test Ether. We will create a smart contract, which itself releases tokens when money is transferred to it. In order to get tokens we need to send Ether to the address of the contract, tokens will come in response. The money for the tokens will be transferred to the owner of the Smart Contract.

Go to the contracts section and then click Contracts and then click "deploy new contract». Then copy the code from the link with the name Test SM Code and insert the contract code into the SOLIDITY CONTRACT SOURCE CODE section. On the right in the drop-down list, select the item as in the example, and fill in the fields using the same principle.

Your Smart Contract is ready!

Even though it may seem that issuing tokens is quite simple as well as creating Smart Contracts on Ethereum, I recommend that you contact qualified experts. They will help to develop various scenarios of Smart Contracts directly for your business model.

The next step is the technical audit of your Smart Contracts for which the contract code must be available on Github.

Technological audit of Smart-Contracts

The main value of Smart Contract is also the main

threat. Smart Contract with vulnerability will work against the one who created it. To reduce risks, it is necessary to audit smart contracts for vulnerabilities and errors in the code.

External audit can ensure that your contracts function as you expect and will not lead to unfortunate consequences.

Audit will help to identify errors in the code, vulnerabilities, check the logic of the program. A professional and high-quality audit will save your nerves and resources. Even a minor error or defect in the logic of a smart contract can lead to a loss of big money.

If you still doubt, here are a few figures: $ 53 million. It was stolen from The DAO project because of a technical mistake in the code of the smart contract. $ 30 million was stolen because of vulnerability in Ethereum-wallet Parity. For the same reason, the Satoshi Pie fund lost 32.4% of its assets. And there are many such examples.

There are many services on the market that help to conduct external audit. You can find a contractor by feedback on the Bitcointalk forum or to Google "audit of Smart Contracts».

Anti-fishing & Blockchain Cybersecurity Rules

According to the analytical agency Chainalysis, since early 2017 hackers have stolen about 10% of funds directed at the ICO. For the year, investors lost about $ 225 million in funds due to fishing schemes.

The most common hacking schemes are:

- Scammers register the same domain in another zone and completely clone your website. They also clone the repository on GitHub. During the ICO, they organize a DDOS attack on your site and when it stops working, they spread a link to all the public records and chat rooms to fishing, stating that there is a mirror working there and you can pay. And investors pay, but not to you but to scammers;
- Creation of fishing sites - copies of the official resource ICO Crowd sale with other people's wallets;
- Use of the vulnerabilities of the site or web application to replace wallets or theft of funds;
- Attacks through company employees;
- Unauthorized operations (fraud).

How to anticipate the actions of intruders?

- Register all similar domains,
- Monitor GitHub and look for Google's similar names, which can be fishing;
- Using DDoS Prevention: connect an intermediate CDN service (for example Cloud flare);
- Conduct audit of smart contracts 5-6 times,
- Deny any links or publications of any addresses in groups and chats;
- Test the IT infrastructure for penetration (Penetration Test);
- Integration of the Web Application Firewall is important;
- Anti-fishing bot for Slack and other messengers;
- Detecting and blocking fishing is round-the-clock monitoring and prompt response to the appearance of fishing resources, unauthorized contextual advertising, e-mail newsletters, accounts in social networks and channels in instant messaging using

your brand;
- The main thing is to use complex secure passwords.

ICO Support

Since the beginning of the Pre-ICO it is necessary to organize a round-the-clock duty of a specialist from each direction.

You need to be in touch with your users round the clock, moderate the branches of forums, make sure that scammers do not replace tread on the forums. And most importantly, monitor the efficiency of your site and the safety of funds on wallets.

At the time of your launch, hackers can hack your site and replace your wallet numbers with theirs , thus capturing the funds from users which were for you. It happens frequently during the ICO.

For the organization of technical support, you need to:

1. Form an expert team.
2. Create and constantly update the FAQ lists.
3. Respond to questions 24/7 from users on all possible channels (Forums, Reddit, Slack, Social Networks, Messengers).

TOKEN SALE

Instruction for buyers of the token

The person who first collides with the logic of crypto-currency, from the first time understands little. Bad, if such a person is your potential investor, who needs to buy FIAT crypto-currencies to invest in you.

To simplify the purchase of your token, you need to take care of detailed instructions for buying a token.

Attention: you need to create a step-by-step instruction with graphical illustrations. The instruction should consist of at least 2 parts: the first part for holders of FIAT Money, the second part for the holders of Cryptocurrency.

Approximate content of the instruction:

- Date and time of the start of the Pre-ICO / ICO;
- Instructions for installing a crypto-currency wallet (for example, Metamask or Mist) with a download link;
- Account registration in the wallet;

- A warning about the importance of saving a password;
- Steps for the purchase of Ethereum / Bitcoin, etc. cryptocurrency for FIAT;
- Checking the receipt of the purchased crypto currency in the wallet;
- Sending funds to the personal cabinet of the ICO site (or direct purchase of the token);
- Steps to buy a token from your personal cabinet;
- Steps for the release of the token from the personal cabinet to the wallet.

Token Crowdsale

So, finally the long-awaited day has come. You have prepared marketing, made a website, connected crypto-currency wallets, prepared tokens and developed smart contracts, your investors are ready, the team is tired but ready to continue to conquer the peaks.

And the counter starts ICO beats the mark of 00 days 00 hours 00 minutes 00 seconds.

And what should you do at that moment? This is the most crucial moment. Contrary to popular belief, work does not end here, but rather intensifies. You need to be even stronger on marketing, attracting new investors, cybersecurity and Support.

Your PR team at this point should splash in the metrics of fees of your ICO into the media, how many investors invested in the first hour, for the first day, how much money was raised. For sure during this period you will have the most unforeseen circumstances.

Do not be lazy to wrap them in a humorous cover and write about them on blogs, in Blockchain Media. Share experiences, cases, figures, show that you like to solve difficulties and your team is ready for anything.

Direct all possible energy to increase the reach of potential audience, and at the same time, as never before, observe the precautionary measures!

After the end of the ICO, you will repeatedly count the fees in all crypto-currencies and FIAT, lost or stolen funds, and form the balance of your ICO, according to which you will give each investor tokens they deserve.

If your tokens cost a fixed amount, and you collected Soft Cap and did not reach Hard Cap, you might need to take care of paying off the underpaid tokens.

Pay to your investors and take a day off, you deserve it ☺

Storage and Transfer of Funds received by ICO

It is better to use Multisignature Wallets for the maximum safety of storing your collected funds.

If the collected amounts are quite impressive, you should think about splitting the sum into several wallets. Storage of tokens at founders' can also be carried out using Trezor's secure hardware purse.

Never use hot wallets to store crypto currency and a significant number of tokens. Be aware of keeping funds on the wallets of exchanges, do not repeat our mistakes.

Holders of your ERC20 assets can store and manage purchased tokens using existing Ethereum clients, including the official Ethereum wallet Mist, MyEtherWallet.com, Plugin Metamask or the same hardware wallet Trezor.

After ICO

Congratulations!
You have gone through the hard way of crowdfunding, for a few months decided the scope of tasks, which in normal circumstances takes about a year, and collected the desired funds, hopefully!

What's next? Next you have to fulfil your obligations to investors. This is the most important part of the ICO model because the viability of the ICO model depends on how successful the ICO-implemented projects will be.

Spend the funds received solely for the intended purpose, remember that each transaction in Blockchain is transparent and easily tracked even by an unprepared user. Move forward, do not forget about Lean Startup and Customer Development.

I wish you success in the implementation of your ICO and the subsequent development of the project.

HOW TO LAUNCH A SUCCESSFUL ICO? FULL ICO CHECKLIST

Initial Coin Offering Campaign Checklist. 111 important points

1. Take from 3 (the minimum) to 8 months for preparation for the ICO.
2. Make sure that the start of your ICO and holding it does not happen at the time of long holidays or a vacation season.
3. Think of a new viable idea of a future breakthrough product. What problem does your idea solve? How many people in the world are experiencing the same problem?
4. Get together the people with the same understanding (key members) to the team.
5. Consider a technical solution for implementing your idea.
6. Study the market, who has already solved this problem in the traditional market as well as in the Blockchain industry.

7. Study the 10-20 last successful ICOs.
8. Study the discussions of the latest ICO in the BitcoinTalk forum.
9. Learn White Paper of the popular ICOs. Pay attention to the depth of study, structure and design.
10. Study the market in your niche: the volume of the market, the dynamics of growth of the market.
11. Put the idea into a business project - work out the primary economic model of the idea.
12. Justify the interest in the project from the market - why the market will be interested in your development?
13. Think of the first (possibly temporary) name for your project.
14. Place the Pre-announcement. Discuss your idea with Blockchain Community, for example, on BitcoinTalk.
15. Finalize the idea after receiving feedback from the community.
16. Develop a business model for your project. A good example of visualization is the Business Model Canvas.
17. Calculate the financial model of your project. Involve an expert on Financial modeling.
18. Determine, what amount of collected funds the campaign is considered successful at? What size Soft Cap (and possibly Hard Cap) to attract? Is there a return if the goal is not reached?
19. Work out models of using the token inside the project.
20. Think of the name and the ticker for a token / tokens.
21. Determine the amount produced by tokens.
22. Develop a model for the distribution of tokens between the team, large investors and the open market.
23. Determine the primary cost of the token.

24. Begin negotiations with the exchange on the withdrawal of your token. Prepare the feasibility of the demand potential for a token.

25. Develop the rules of the game for investors, the size of the discount for the first investors, etc.

26. Decide whether to accept investments from citizens of the United States, Singapore and other countries with strict regulation?

27. Determine the geography of the ICO.

28. Identify the models of smart contracts. Describe their scenarios.

29. Decide which types of crypto-currency you will collect during the ICO (Bitcoin, Ethereum, or something different?). Will you sell a token for Fiat? If so, how to buy a token for Fiat money?

30. On which platform will the tokens be issued?

31. Determine whether you will run Pre-ICO or immediately start ICO? Will it be Private or Public Pre-ICO? How much funds do you plan to raise? What are the dates of the event? What will the first investors receive and on what terms? How many tokens will be released?

32. Develop the Timeline of the entire ICO. Take time for preparation, the interval of several months between Pre-ICO and ICO.

33. Decide whether you need a Bounty program? What are the conditions of a bounty program? Make a list of works and develop a technical assignment.

34. After the completion of the ICO: where will the collected funds go to? Are there different development models depending on the amount of funds collected?

35. Demonstrate to the community which exchanges preliminary agreements on the listing of the token have been reached with and indicate the timing of the listing.

36. Conduct an audit of your project (or its source code) by independent auditors. Place the source code on the GitHub.
37. Work out a model of protection of your investors with Escrow.
38. Develop a strategic development plan for your product and draw a Roadmap.
39. Form the ICO Timeline.
40. Bring in all the specialists who you lack, into the team, at the stage to prepare for the further conduct of the ICO.
41. Prepare an Executive Summary.
42. Make a draft of ICO WhitePaper.
43. Involve Advisors.
44. Start negotiations with major strategic investors.
45. Prepare a specialist to work with Community management and Bounty.
46. Start attracting Bounty specialists.
47. Start to actively involve the community.
48. Develop the final Naming of your project. Buy domains.
49. Develop Brand book & Design Templates.
50. Draw all the pictures, charts and diagrams.
51. Develop a site structure.
52. Draw a design and make a website.
53. Make video interviews and videos.
54. Work on (on the site and in PDF) the Guide page where you describe How to participate in the Your Token Sale.
55. Get a blog of the project, pages in social media and instant messengers.
56. Develop a chain of letters for Email marketing.
57. Find a qualified Blockchain lawyer.
58. Work out the jurisdiction for your ICO.
59. Negotiate with banks for a preliminary agreement to open an account.

60. Work out the Know Your Customer model (KYC).
61. Study the tax aspects of potential jurisdictions for ICO.
62. Optimize the tax scheme.
63. Determine the legal essence of the token.
64. Check the token on Securities.
65. Develop all legal documents.
66. Work out the organizational structure of the company.
67. Select jurisdiction and register the company, holding or SPV.
68. Register a bank account. Do not forget to work out a legal model of involving or excluding offers from citizens of Singapore, USA, Puerto Rico, Virgin Islands of the United States and other dependent territories of the United States.
69. Prepare an Offer for investors.
70. Select and create a secure Multi-sig Wallet.
71. Attract guarantors to Escrow.
72. Involve Blockchain developers for Smart Contracts & Tokens.
73. Choose a platform for releasing tokens.
74. Develop Smart-Contracts.
75. Prepare Tokens emission.
76. Prepare the project for Due Diligence.
77. Run several iterations of the technological audit of Smart-Contracts.
78. Involve a CyberSecurity Specialist
79. Develop the mechanics of Anti-Phishing protection.
80. Start the Support service.
81. Bring qualified marketers and PR specialists.
82. Prepare all the project descriptions.
83. Determine Target Audience for your ICO.
84. Develop a media plan.
85. Conduct a basic SEO site.
86. Register on ICO tracking.

87. Start PR activities.
88. Work out the popular Tech Blogs.
89. Enable Blockchain Forums and blogs.
90. Connect Reddit.
91. Start SMM on Facebook, LinkedIn and Instagram.
92. Start promoting the Youtube channel.
93. Do streaming broadcasting & Live videos on Facebook and Instagram.
94. Start Email Marketing.
95. Include contextual advertising with Google, Bing and Yahoo.
96. Constantly write articles, shoot videos and use Content Marketing.
97. Publish videos and interviews at a given periodicity throughout the preparation period for the ICO.
98. Start buying Targeted Blockchain Traffic.
99. Connect Google Ad words and measure the conversion.
100. Get chat bots.
101. Constantly place all information about the project on profile sites, in groups as well as in chats.
102. Participate in conferences.
103. Organize Meet ups and Workshops.
104. Announce start-up competitions and competitions on ICO.
105. Involve Blockchain enthusiasts.
106. Make to crypto-currency and investment funds. Tell them your metrics.
107. On the selected day, start Pre-ICO or Token Crowdsale (ICO).
108. Monitor the security of the Storage of Funds received by ICO.
109. Complete your ICO with thanks to everyone who believes in you.
110. Fulfill all these promises.
111. Constantly develop your product.

Links

Cryptocurrency Market Capitalizations & Exchange Rates
https://coinmarketcup.com

Popular Cryptocurrency Trading Platforms
https://www.coinbase.com
https://www.bitfinex.com
https://poloniex.com
https://www.kraken.com
https://paxful.com
https://bittrex.com
https://www.bitstamp.net
https://cex.io/buysell
https://localbitcoins.com
https://yobit.net/en
https://blockchain.info
https://www.coinmama.com
https://etherdelta.com

Cryptocurrency Exchanger
https://shapeshift.io

Аналитика рынка ICO
https://www.smithandcrown.com/

Crypto Valley
https://cryptovalley.swiss

Blockcihan Ethereum
https://etherscan.io/

Blockchain Bitcoin
http://blockchain.info

Wallets
Mist https://github.com/ethereum/mist/releases
Metamask
https://chrome.google.com/webstore/detail/metamask/n
kbihfbeogaeaoehlefnkodbefgpgknn

ICO Trackers
icoalert.com
icorating.com
ratei.co
icobounce.com
Cyber.fund/radar
Icocountdown.com
Smithandcrown.com
The-blockchain.com
Coinschedule.com
Icotracker.net
Tokenmarket.net
Tokenhub.com
Cointelegraph.com
Ico-list.com
Icobazaar.com
Coingecko.com

Token Generation ERC20 Description
https://github.com/ethereum/EIPs/issues/20

Geth
https://github.com/ethereum/go-ethereum/wiki/geth

Source of Cryptocurrency & Tokens
https://www.ethereum.org/token

Token Generation manual
https://blog.ethereum.org/2015/12/03/how-to-build-
your-own-cryptocurrency/

Custom Token Code
https://ethereum.github.io/browser-
solidity/#version=soljson-v0.4.18+commit.9cf6e910.js

Repository
https://github.com
https://bitbucket.org

DDoS Safety
https://www.cloudflare.com

All traffic generators
https://cointraffic.io/
http://coinad.com/
https://bitmedia.io
http://www.adhitz.com/
https://coinurl.com/index.php
http://btcclicks.com/

Successful ICO online Course
https://goo.gl/V1KRmq

Services for accounting of tax base
https://bitcoin.tax/
http://www.libra.tech/
https://www.kryptofolio-tax.com/

ABOUT THE AUTHOR

The serial entrepreneur, technological expert and producer. Organizer of technology conferences, educational events, and business accelerators. The author of innovative projects and strategies for economic development. Lived in Asia, Europe, and North America. Founded a charity project to support start-ups. Currently focused on the study of the digital economy, the development of breakthrough technologies and on the educational project EduTelly.com

.

Made in the USA
Coppell, TX
10 April 2021

53441891R00080